JOHN LEWIS

JOHN LEWIS
THE LAST INTERVIEW
and OTHER CONVERSATIONS

with an introduction by JELANI COBB

MELVILLE HOUSE
BROOKLYN • LONDON

Melville House Publishing   Suite 2000
46 John Street   and   16/18 Woodford Road
Brooklyn, NY 11201   London E7 0HA

mhpbooks.com
@melvillehouse

ISBN: 978-1-61219-962-7
ISBN: 978-1-61219-963-4 (eBook)

Printed in the United States of America

1   3   5   7   9   10   8   6   4   2

A catalog record for this book is available from the Library of Congress.

CONTENTS

INTRODUCTION

JELANI COBB

For a blessed handful of dreamers life affords the chance to work for great, unrealistic aspirations and witness them as they come to pass. These moments in which history seems to relinquish its grip upon the present and vast new vistas of possibility emerge are rare and invaluable and mark all who live through them. But even the greatest of leaps remain subject to gravity. Frederick Douglass, who audaciously fought to kill the institution of slavery, witnessed the Emancipation Proclamation, the ratification of the Thirteenth Amendment, and the election of over six hundred black people to political office in the decade after the Civil War. But he also saw the tide of retribution that swept the South following the end of Reconstruction, lynching and the brutal reinscription of near-slavery amid the depths of Jim Crow. When a young Black man approached the aged Douglass near the end of his life, asking how he might be of service to his race, Douglass famously replied "Agitate, agitate, agitate." History, he seemed to be saying, is not vanquished so easily.

John Lewis was among that number of blessed Dreamers. And as with Douglass his life afforded him the view of great moral leaps and reiterated the power of gravity. By the time Lewis made his exit from this realm, on July 17, 2020, his life had been bound so tightly and for so long to the mythos of the movement for democracy in America that it was difficult to separate him from it. For this reason, a friend who texted me "John Lewis is gone, what are we going to do now?" was not only reacting to grief but expressing a real and common sentiment. Lewis, who spoke at the March on Washington, chaired the Student Nonviolent Coordinating Committee, and served seventeen terms in Congress, representing Georgia's Fifth District, succumbed to pancreatic cancer, a ruthless and efficient plague whose diagnosis is fatal around 95 percent of the time. When he revealed his condition last December, hope persisted despite those odds, in part because, for many people, the thought of confronting the reactionary, racist, and antidemocratic realities of the Trump era without one of the nation's most potent symbols of decency was simply too difficult to countenance.

Those contrasts were not merely hypothetical. In 2017, when President Trump announced that he would attend the opening of the Mississippi Civil Rights Museum, Lewis said that he would not. In a fit of absurdism the then–White House press secretary, Sarah Huckabee Sanders, criticized Lewis of failing to show proper respect for the movement. Months earlier, Trump had attacked Georgia's Fifth Congressional District, which Lewis represented, as "crime-infested" and suggested that the blame lay with the Congressman. I wrote at the time that Trump's disdain for Lewis betrayed a theme: Having never grasped the concept of sacrifice, the President is contemptuous of people whose lives have been defined by it. No criticism that Lewis issued about Trump was as strong an indictment as the simple facts of his life: born to Alabama sharecroppers, stalwart of SNCC, leader, exemplar of humility.

The civil rights movement is best understood as a collaboration between two groups of people: the martyrs who died for the cause, and the stalwarts who were tasked with living for it. The first group is most commonly associated with Martin Luther King Jr., whose death, at the hands of an assassin, cleaved an entire section of American history into before and after. But a different, strange, and particular burden befell the second group, the people who survived the manifold dangers of Albany, Anniston, Jackson, and Little Rock, and were then witness to the trials of crack and AIDS, violence, and mass incarceration. They were tasked with institutionalizing and defending the movement's hard-won gains against the slow accretion of power by people who hoped to remake the present in the image of the past. Lewis, like his peers Andrew Young, Marion Barry, and Eleanor Holmes Norton, transitioned into elected office as the post from which he would undertake this work. It was not an easy undertaking.

. . .

John Lewis ran for Congress in 1986, in a race that pitted him against his former SNCC colleague Julian Bond, by then a Georgia state senator who was well connected in the district and heavily favored to win. Lewis prevailed in a bitter contest, in which, reportedly to make fighting drug abuse an issue in the campaign, he challenged Bond to take a drug test. (Bond said that it would trivialize the issue.) The bare-knuckles politicking was a departure for Lewis, who, throughout his tenure in the civil rights movement and his time as the chairman of SNCC, had been thought of as "too nice." The fact was, though, that there had always been political infighting in the movement. In 1966, Lewis was ousted as SNCC chairman by Stokely Carmichael, a brilliant orator whose militant politics were to the left of Lewis's and more reflective of the emerging radical zeitgeist. Even decades later, Lewis referred to the move as "almost like a coup."

The politics of the movement surfaced again, in 2008, when I interviewed Lewis about the possibility of the first Black president being elected. The conversation turned to Lewis's role in the 1963 March on Washington. He was by that time the last surviving speaker from the event, and he recalled how his speech, a firebrand condemnation of the Democratic Party that culminated in a pledge to "march through the South, through the heart of Dixie, the way Sherman did" and "burn Jim Crow to the ground—nonviolently," had alarmed the other participants so much that several refused to participate if he gave it. The impasse was resolved when King personally oversaw a more conciliatory edit of the address.

The story was significant as part of Lewis's first-person
narrative of the movement, but it also implicitly served another purpose. Lewis had been harshly criticized in his district
for supporting Hillary Clinton over Barack Obama during
the 2008 Democratic Presidential primaries. Lewis was a
superdelegate and not bound to support the same candidate
as his district, which voted overwhelmingly for Obama. The
old criticism of Lewis being too moderate for the moment
had resurfaced and, in reminding me of that moment in 1963,
he was subtly pointing to the fact that he had not been too
moderate to nearly get himself killed on behalf of his constituents before many of them had even been born. It was not
insignificant that Lewis was associated with a specific theatre
of the struggle and a particular instance of brutality. He was
among the marchers attacked at the Edmund Pettus Bridge
during the "Bloody Sunday" demonstrations in Selma, Alabama, that were part of the campaign for a national voting-
rights act. He wrote of the moment in his memoir *Walking
with the Wind*, from 1998:

> The first of the troopers came over me, a large, husky
> man. Without a word, he swung his club against the left
> side of my head. I didn't feel any pain, just the thud of
> the blow and my legs giving way. I raised an arm—a re-
> flex motion—as I curled up in the "prayer for protection"
> position. And then the same trooper hit me again. And
> everything started to spin.

Lewis, who was bleeding badly, somehow made it back
across the bridge. He returned to the church that had been

a staging area for the march and gave a speech denouncing
Lyndon B. Johnson's priorities. "I don't know how President
Johnson can send troops to Vietnam, I don't see how he can
send troops to the Congo, I don't see how he can send troops
to Africa, and can't send troops to Selma," he said.

The footage of brutal bedlam in Selma pressured Johnson to support what eventually became the Voting Rights Act
of 1965. There had already been a great deal of blood spilled
in pursuit of justice: two years earlier, the SCLC activist An-
nell Ponder and SNCC activist Fannie Lou Hamer had been
arrested along with three others and beaten, Hamer by male
prison inmates at the behest of the white guards; Andrew
Goodman, James Chaney, and Michael Schwerner had already been murdered near Philadelphia, Mississippi; and Jim-
mie Lee Jackson, an activist with the Selma campaign, had
been killed by an Alabama police officer just a month earlier.
But a relationship between the bloodshed at the bridge and
the signature legislation was cinched as cause and effect in
both the history and the mythology of the movement.

It then fell to Lewis to serve as the guardian of the legislation each time it came up for renewal in Congress. It's
therefore difficult to reconcile the present state of the Voting Rights Act—gutted by the Supreme Court's 2013 Shelby
County v. Holder decision, which nonetheless left an av-
enue to reinstate key sections of the law should Congress
author a suitable revision of it—and the posthumous praise
for Lewis that emanated from the Republicans who have
refused to support it. Senate Majority Leader Mitch Mc-
Connell tweeted his fond remembrance of singing "We Shall
Overcome" with Lewis, a claim that immediately suggests

that McConnell should have been singing that song in the second person. Lewis was too good a man to be praised by Mitch McConnell.

The question posed as the news of Lewis's death broke remains: What exactly does one do when a figure of his stature departs? The answer may be in the last public image we have of Lewis. Last month, weakened by illness but still standing, his face obscured by a mask but still unmistakable as himself, he inspected the huge words painted on the street in front of the White House: BLACK LIVES MATTER. His posture reiterated the charge: agitate, agitate, agitate. Terminal cancer could not stop him from paying homage to the movement that was continuing the work to which he'd devoted his life. What do we do now, we asked. His posture answered for him as he stood wordlessly on the street, telling us that you grieve, you endure, you agitate, then you do more of the same.

JOHN LEWIS

WILLIAMS V. WALLACE

INTERVIEW BY PETER A. HALL, JACK GREENBERG,
NORMAN AMAKER, AND CHARLES H. JONES, JR.,
ATTORNEYS FOR THE PLAINTIFF AND MAURY D. SMITH,
W. MCLEAN PITTS ATTORNEYS FOR THE
DEFENDANT US DISTRICT COURT FOR THE MIDDLE
DISTRICT OF ALABAMA
MARCH 17, 1965

John Lewis, a Plaintiff, having been duly sworn, testified as follows:

DIRECT EXAMINATION BY MR. [PETER A.] HALL

HALL: State your name, occupation, and address, please?

LEWIS: I am John Lewis, National Chairman of the Student Nonviolent Coordinating Committee, native of Troy, Alabama, and I live at Atlanta, Georgia.

HALL: Are you one of the plaintiffs in this case?

LEWIS: I am.

HALL: Would you tell us what you do, Mr. Lewis?

LEWIS: I am the Chairman of the Nonviolent Coordinating Committee.

HALL: You are the National Chairman?

LEWIS: Right.

HALL: Will you tell us what Student Nonviolent Coordinating Committee is?

LEWIS: The Student Nonviolent Coordinating Committee is one of the civil rights organizations. It is for the interracial organization working in the South to bring an interracial democracy through nonviolent, direct action and political action and political education. We was organized in 1960, and we have been working for some months in—and years in the State of Alabama.

HALL: Have you been working in Dallas County, Alabama?

LEWIS: We have been working in Dallas County since January 1963.

HALL: Have you also been working in Perry and Marengo, Hale, and adjacent counties?

LEWIS: We have been working in Perry and other Black Belt counties near Dallas.

HALL: What is the nature of your activities in Dallas and adjacent counties, sir?

LEWIS: Well, since January 1963, on invitation by the Dallas County Voters League, we have been conducting voter registration workshops, clinics, assisting in organizing mass meetings, encouraging people to go down to the county courthouse and attempt to register to vote.

HALL: Has your organization sponsored house-to-house canvasses, too?

LEWIS: We have participated in house-to-house canvasses, that is, knocking on doors, making surveys, find out how many people registered, how many people not registered, and encouraging people to go down and attempt to register.

HALL: Has your organization engaged in any demonstrations, marches?

LEWIS: We have engaged in nonviolent demonstrations, nonviolent marches to the Dallas County Courthouse.

HALL: As a result of such demonstrations and marches, have you or any of your workers been beaten by the police?

LEWIS: Well, I have been arrested and also beaten in Dallas County.

HALL: Would you tell us about this arrest, how these arrests and these beatings—When was the first one, first arrest?

MAURY D. SMITH: We object, if the court please.

HALL: Beg your pardon?

SMITH: We object to this.

THE COURT: To his having been beaten?

SMITH: Says "when was the first arrest"; [it] isn't related in point of time. Of course, I guess the answer would tell us that; I withdraw it until he gives it.

THE COURT: He went in January '63; I will permit it; overrule.

LEWIS: My first arrest occurred in Selma, in Dallas County, at the county courthouse on September 25, 1963.

SMITH: We object to this, if the court please.

W. MCLEAN PITTS: What I want to object to is that there are several cases pending before—I don't think he is a plaintiff in one of them or not, but there are several cases pending in the Southern District where all of this stuff is gone into, and the Student Nonviolent Coordinating Committee, and I think John Lewis—was he one of the plaintiffs?

HALL: I think he might be.

PITTS: I am not sure whether he was or not, but all this stuff was gone into, and then in addition to that, in your three-judge district court case in Selma, a good bit of this was gone into. That is—I don't think it pertains to this march.

THE COURT: I understand the legal principles that are controlling in this case presently being heard and before me involve generally a balancing of rights; as I thought I made clear yesterday, I was going to permit a certain amount of history on both sides, as far as the demonstrations and the reasons for the demonstrations and the extent of any mistreatment that—that they complain of, and that is the reason that I am going to admit it.

HALL: Mr. Lewis, did your organization participate in an attempted march from Selma to Montgomery, Alabama, on Sunday, March 7, 1965?

LEWIS: We did participate in attempted march from Selma to Montgomery on March 7, 1965.

HALL: Did you, yourself, participate in this attempted march?

LEWIS: I did.

HALL: Were you one of the leaders of the march?

LEWIS: Hosea Williams and I was at the front of the line.

HALL: I show you, Mr. Lewis, a photograph marked Plaintiffs' Exhibit 4, and ask you if you can identify it for us, sir?

LEWIS: Yes, I can.

HALL: Can you tell us what it is?

LEWIS: This photograph is a scene where state troopers are pushing and tramping and beating some of us that was in the line, and I see myself is here, and a state trooper is standing over me.

HALL: And this is a true likeness of what occurred at that time?

LEWIS: It is.

HALL: Mr. Lewis, I show you a photograph marked Plaintiffs' Exhibit 5 for identification, ask you to examine it and see if you can identify it?

LEWIS: I can identify this photograph.

HALL: Can you tell us what it is?

LEWIS: It is the line of march being rushed back, beat down by a line of state troopers; I see Mr. Hosea Williams on the ground, and I see where a state trooper has just hit me, and I have my hand up like this [*demonstrates*].

HALL: And this is a true likeness of what happened at that time?

LEWIS: A true likeness; yes, sir.

HALL: Were you, on Sunday, March 7, 1965, allowed to go across the [Edmund] Pettus Bridge in Selma in your attempt to march to Montgomery?

LEWIS: Yes.

HALL: How many persons were in that line, in your best judgment?

LEWIS: I would say between 650 and 700.

HALL: Did—and you and—Mr. Williams and you, as you have said, were in front of the line?

LEWIS: Right.

HALL: You got across the bridge; is that correct?

LEWIS: Right.

HALL: In your best judgment, how far across the bridge did you get?

LEWIS: I would say we moved about a block and a half or two blocks beyond the bridge.

HALL: Will you tell the court what then happened?

LEWIS: About fifty feet away from the line of state troopers, a state trooper wearing a state trooper—

HALL: May I interrupt you just a moment?

LEWIS: Uh-huh.

HALL: Do I understand you to say there were some state troopers?

LEWIS: Right; before we crossed the bridge, we could see a line of state troopers.

HALL: In your best judgment, how many troopers did you see?

LEWIS: Well, I saw many, and it would be very hard and difficult for me to—

HALL: You have no judgment as to how many?

LEWIS: I would say between eighty and a hundred.

HALL: Where were these troopers stationed?

LEWIS: Some were standing across the highway all the way across; others were standing on the side; there was others in the background.

HALL: How close did you approach to these officers before your line stopped?

LEWIS: We were able to move about fifty feet, and at that time a state trooper made an announcement on a bullhorn or megaphone, and he said, "This march will not continue."

HALL: What happened then? Did the line stop?

LEWIS: The line stopped at that time.

HALL: You stopped still?

LEWIS: Yes, sir.

HALL: You didn't advance any further?

LEWIS: We stopped right then.

HALL: Then what happened?

LEWIS: He said, "I am Major Cloud, and this is an unlawful assembly. This demonstration will not continue. You have been banned by the governor. I am going to order you to disperse.

HALL: What did you then do?

LEWIS: Mr. Williams said, "Mr. Major, I would like to have a word, can we have a word?" And he said, "No, I will give you two minutes to leave." And again Mr. Williams said, "Can I have a word?" He said, "There will be no word." And about a minute or more Major Cloud ordered the troopers to advance, and at that time the state troopers took their position, I guess, and they moved forward with their clubs up over their—near their shoulder, the top part of the body; they came rushing in, knocking us down and pushing us.

HALL: And were you hit at that time?

LEWIS: At that time I was hit and knocked down.

HALL: Where were you hit?

LEWIS: I was hit on my head right here [*gestures*].

HALL: What were you hit with?

LEWIS: I was hit with a billy club, and I saw the state trooper that hit me.

HALL: How many times were you hit?

LEWIS: I was hit twice, once when I was lying down and was attempting to get up.

HALL: Do we understand you to say you were hit and then attempted to get up and was hit again is that correct?

LEWIS: [*Nods.*]

HALL: Can you identify the trooper who hit you?

LEWIS: I am not positive that I could identify the trooper from the picture I—I can identify the trooper from the picture.

HALL: Were you knocked unconscious?

LEWIS: I was not knocked unconscious.

HALL: Did you see other people around you hit?

LEWIS: I saw other people that was behind me hit and knocked down; I did see them.

HALL: Were any words said by the troopers?

LEWIS: Well, the troopers, most of them kept saying, "Move back, move back, you niggers, disperse," and calling people Black bitches and son of bitches and things like that.

HALL: Did you see any of the marchers use any violence at all in an effort to defend themselves or to fight the police officers?

LEWIS: There was no act of violence or any type of retaliation, rather retaliatory acts, on the part of any of the demonstrators.

HALL: After you were stopped, at some subsequent time was tear gas used by the state troopers, or some form of gas?

LEWIS: Well, when we were forced back, most of the people in line kneeling in a prayerful manner; they had back toward Selma, kneeling, the line all the way back was almost a spontaneous reaction on the part of all the people in the line as far back as you could see, and at that time the major ordered the trooper to put on their gas masks, and they started throwing gas, and people became sick and started vomiting, and some of us was forced off of the highway and behind some buildings in the woods.

HALL: Did you see Sheriff James Clark on that side of the bridge at that time or at any time during this happening?

LEWIS: I didn't see Sheriff Clark at that particular time. On the way back into Selma, I saw Sheriff Clark in his car going across the bridge.

HALL: Going across the bridge?

LEWIS: Back into Selma.

HALL: You saw James—Sheriff Clark—come across the bridge into Selma?

LEWIS: Right.

HALL: Did you see any of the sheriff's deputies across the bridge? At the time you saw the state troopers?

LEWIS: I saw some of the sheriff's deputies, I saw at least one rider on a horseback, and I know this one very well, because

I have seen him in the courtroom many, many times in the county courthouse in Selma.

HALL: In Selma; you saw this man on a horse on the east side of the river?

LEWIS: Right; he was on the bridge.

HALL: Where the incident occurred, did you see any other mounted officers?

LEWIS: No.

HALL: Officers mounted on horseback?

LEWIS: I saw many members of the posse* that I have recognized from previous occasions riding horses.

HALL: Well, what were they doing over there?

LEWIS: On the way back and across the bridge, members of the posse would get—would attempt to make the horse get on the sidewalk to the walkway on the bridge, and they would force people, they would get between the group of marchers, and they would run the horses up near the people, and at one time one of the posses made the horse rear back and start pawing people in the back, and they start taking whips and bullwhips,

---

* Members of the Ku Klux Klan and its supporters organized by Sheriff Jim Clark in response to the Student Nonviolent Coordinating Committee's (SNCC) voting drives.

and the whips about eight to ten feet long, beating people, and I saw one incident, myself, where a member of the posse start beating a Negro woman, she dropped her bag, she lost her shoes and everything, she was trying to run, and she sort of turned around and stared at the posseman who was beating her, and he said, "Get on, you Black nigger woman, you."

HALL: Were you able, Mr. Lewis, to walk back to the church?

LEWIS: Well, I was able to walk back, but with the aid and assistance of some of our staff people and other people that was in the line.

HALL: By aid and assistance, do you mean that they partially supported you?

LEWIS: Right.

HALL: So you were able to get on back to the church. Now, did you observe any police activity on the way back to the church?

LEWIS: All the way back to the church there was hundreds of marchers, people who had been in the march line, women, men, children, that was forced back toward the church. Some was running, because the posse or riding horses, some running through the streets, were running them down, and people was running for safety toward the church.

HALL: Did you see any of the Dallas County deputy sheriffs?

LEWIS: I did. They were engaged in the same type of activity that the members of the posse was engaged in.

HALL: And you went on back to the church. Now, did you at some subsequent time lose consciousness or become ill?

LEWIS: I did not lose conscious; I arrived back at the church, and I spoke to the group at the church; some of the people had gathered, some of the people had remained at the church; for about two minutes, and while I was speaking I began to feel sharp pains in the head and felt very bad, and I went next door and was assisted and aided next door in the parsonage by some members of the medical committee and Dr. Dinkins, and they recommended that I be sent to the Good Samaritan, and later an ambulance took me to Good Samaritan Hospital.

HALL: And were you hospitalized there; how long did you stay there?

LEWIS: I stayed there from late Sunday afternoon until early Tuesday morning.

HALL: Do you have any knowledge as to the initial diagnosis on your admittance at Good Samaritan?

LEWIS: Well, on Sunday evening they made some X-ray of my head, and the doctor informed me that it was possible a fractured skull.

HALL: This was ruled out later on, is that correct?

LEWIS: Right.

HALL: How long were you there at the Good Samaritan Hospital?

LEWIS: Until early Tuesday morning.

HALL: That's all.

CROSS EXAMINATION BY MR. [MAURY D.] SMITH

SMITH: You say you are a National Chairman of the Student Nonviolent Coordinating Committee?

LEWIS: I am.

SMITH: How long have you held this position?

LEWIS: Since June of 1963 I have been Chairman of the Student Nonviolent Coordinating Committee.

SMITH: How long have you known Dr. Martin Luther King?

LEWIS: I have known of Dr. Martin Luther King since 1955; I got to know him in 1958.

SMITH: Where did you get to know Dr. King?

LEWIS: Well, I met Dr. King at mass meetings, and here in the city of Montgomery.

SMITH: Here in Montgomery; and have you been more or less identified with the civil rights movement since 1955?

LEWIS: Well, I would say that I have been more or less identified with the civil rights movement since the spring of 1960.

SMITH: Since 1960. What is the connection or relationship, if any, between the Student Nonviolent Coordinating Committee and the Southern Christian Leadership Conference?

LEWIS: The Student Nonviolent Coordinating Committee and the Southern Christian Leadership Conference are two separate organizations.

SMITH: They are two separate and more or less distinct organizations?

LEWIS: Right.

SMITH: Is the leadership or the directorate of these organizations interlocked in any way?

LEWIS: The leadership of both organizations are different.

SMITH: Different, right. Now, when did you come to Selma?

LEWIS: I have been in and out of Selma since September of 1963. My first time in Selma, I believe I spoke at a mass meeting there in July '63, but I have been in and out since September 1963.

SMITH: What was the purpose of your being in Selma in September of 1963?

LEWIS: I went there because I was invited by the local citizens of Dallas County, the local citizens of Selma, to speak at a voter registration rally.

SMITH: Was your talk in regard to the voter registration in Dallas County in September 1963?

LEWIS: More or less.

SMITH: What was the purpose of your going to Selma, I believe you said in January of this year?

LEWIS: I didn't say that I went to Selma in January '63; staff members of our organization were invited into Selma in January 1963.

SMITH: Well, did you go there in January of '63?

LEWIS: I did not.

SMITH: When did you go to Selma?

LEWIS: My first—

SMITH: In this year?

LEWIS: I think my first trip into Selma this year was on January 17.

SMITH: Since that date to the present date, have you been more or less continuously in and out of Selma?

LEWIS: I spent over half of my time in the Black Belt area in and around Selma and Dallas County.

SMITH: During that period of time, have there been rallies and marches and mass demonstrations of Negro citizens in regard to voter registration in Dallas County?

LEWIS: There have been voter registration rallies and voter registration demonstrations, and also demonstration to protest police brutality in Selma and Dallas County.

SMITH: Prior to March 7, that would be Sunday of this week, had there been violence in these other mass demonstrations?

LEWIS: There was violence in a mass demonstration in Marion, Alabama.

PITTS: We object to anything concerning Marion or Perry

County, insofar as the defendant Clark is concerned, in that he is not the sheriff of Perry County and has no jurisdiction in Perry County.

THE COURT: Overruled; you can answer it.

LEWIS: Before March 7 there had been violence in Perry County; there has been violence in Selma and Dallas County since September '63; I have witnessed and seen people beaten in and around Dallas County Courthouse in Selma.

SMITH: Now, in the violence which preceded March 7 of this year, in regard to the mass demonstration or marches, did it occur on the streets in Selma?

LEWIS: Well, I have seen violence occur on the streets in Selma, on the part of law enforcement agents.

SMITH: Have any mass demonstrations or marches been held in Selma other than on the streets?

LEWIS: Most of the demonstrations that we have engaged in in Selma have been demonstrations held on the sidewalk, more or less from Brown's Chapel A.M.E. Church to the Dallas County Courthouse.

SMITH: Now, does Selma have areas wherein predominantly members of the Negro race live and certain areas wherein predominantly members of the white race live?

LEWIS: Well, as far as I know the city, there is an area where predominantly members of the Negro race live, and there is an area where many white citizens live like that.

SMITH: That is my question. Have any of these mass demonstrations taken place in the areas of the City of Selma where predominantly the Negro citizens live?

LEWIS: Well, I would say that most of the demonstration originate in the heart of the Negro community in one part of Selma, I guess [the] Brown Chapel A.M.E. Church.

SMITH: From there do they generally, or have they in the past, prior to March 7, proceeded down the public streets into the downtown area?

LEWIS: Down the sidewalk to the Dallas County Courthouse.

SMITH: Now, prior to March 7, where did the violence occur in the other mass demonstrations; did it occur in the areas where the churches are located and where predominantly Negro citizens live, or did it occur in the streets in downtown Selma?

LEWIS: Most of the violence that have occurred, and that was almost all of the violence that have occurred during demonstration or during voter registration demonstration, have occurred near and around the Dallas County Courthouse.

SMITH: Now, when these demonstrations prior to March 7 have taken place, did you observe large numbers of white people standing around the streets observing the demonstration?

LEWIS: On some occasion there have been a few white people, and other occasions there have been more, but on most occasions there since September '63, been relatively few white people standing on the streets.

SMITH: Prior to March 7, have some of these demonstrations attracted large numbers of white people to the downtown area?

LEWIS: I think since September '63, and prior to March 7, that a great many citizens, both Negroes and white, have witnessed the demonstrations.

SMITH: All right; now, you have had considerable experience in mass demonstrations prior to coming to Selma, had you not?

LEWIS: I have been involved in a few.

SMITH: Have you observed crowds of people or masses of people that appeared to be hostile and angry and emotionally pent-up, so to speak?

LEWIS: From time to time I have observed people who are hostile and who happened to be emotion[ally] pent-up.

SMITH: Is it possible, in your judgment, to look at a crowd of people or a mass of people or a gathering of people from a distance and discern whether or not that is a hostile, angry, explosive gathering, as compared to one of peaceful or tranquil meeting?

LEWIS: Well, to a degree, yes; and then to another degree, no. I have seen crowds that have been people who are just concerned and standing there looking in a very orderly and a peaceful manner, on the other hand, I have seen people who are hostile.

SMITH: In other words, you can tell the difference, can't you?

LEWIS: I cannot tell the difference to that degree, because I am not a psychologist.

SMITH: Well, I am not asking for a professional explanation, but you say that you can—you have seen crowds, and some looked peaceful, and you have seen crowds, and some looked hostile?

LEWIS: Well, on occasion I have seen law enforcement people who would stand like they are going to protect people, and they look quite peaceful, peaceable; but at the same time these people have beaten and brutalized people.

SMITH: Prior to March 7, have you seen white citizens in

Selma gathering around or enveloping the area where the Negro mass demonstration are taking place that appeared to be hostile and mad, angry, emotionally upset?

LEWIS: Well, I have not witnessed any large gathering on— no demonstration that I have been on in Selma; I have not witnessed a large gathering of hostile white people in Selma.

SMITH: Well, have you observed any gathering of hostile white people in Selma in connection with the street demonstration of the Negroes?

LEWIS: I have observed—

SMITH: On how many occasions have you observed it prior to March 7 of this year?

LEWIS: I have observed members of the posse, members of the sheriff, members of the sheriff's deputies being hostile [to] people during the demonstration.

SMITH: All right. Now, you were served with a copy of this court's order dated March 9 of this year on the morning of March 9, that Tuesday of this week?

LEWIS: I was not served until late Tuesday evening after the demonstration.

SMITH: Did United States Marshal Arthur Worthy serve you?

LEWIS: I was served by Marshal inside the Brown Chapel A.M.E. Church about four or five p.m. on Tuesday.

SMITH: Was that after the march on Tuesday?

LEWIS: Right.

SMITH: You weren't served with a copy of the order until the march had already taken place?

LEWIS: That's right.

SMITH: Did you know about the order of this court before you were served?

LEWIS: I heard from someone that there was an order, restraining order or injunction.

SMITH: When did you hear that?

LEWIS: I am not sure whether I heard it at the hospital or on my way from the hospital, I am not sure; someone just told me that.

SMITH: Did you know what his order said?

LEWIS: I didn't.

SMITH: Were you told what it said?

LEWIS: Well, I heard in effect that it said that it was prohibiting the attempted march from Selma to Montgomery; I didn't know the exact language or the wording of the order.

SMITH: See if I understand; you heard that Judge Johnson's order prohibited the march from Selma to Montgomery; is that right?

LEWIS: Right.

SMITH: All right. Now, were you in Brown's Chapel on Sylvan Street, I believe at about two o'clock on the afternoon of Tuesday of this week?

LEWIS: I am not sure; I spent a great deal of time at Brown's Chapel A.M.E. Church, and I was in and out of the church and next door to the parsonage, so it is possible that I was there around two o'clock.

SMITH: You and Hosea Williams were the leaders of this march on Tuesday, weren't you?

LEWIS: I did not participate in the march on Tuesday.

SMITH: Were you the leader of the march on Sunday, March 7?

LEWIS: I did participate and was one of the leaders of the march on Sunday, March 7.

SMITH: Were you in the church, on Tuesday afternoon?

LEWIS: I was in the church late Tuesday afternoon; I was there maybe before some of the people left; I am not too sure about that, but I was there when the people returned from the march.

SMITH: How many people, in your judgment, were in the church Tuesday afternoon?

LEWIS: Oh, I would say eight hundred or nine hundred.

SMITH: Did you address this group; did you talk to them?

LEWIS: I am not too sure whether I spoke to the people in the church; I think I said a few word to the people out—

SMITH: I mean to the crowd, I don't mean talking to somebody?

LEWIS: I am not too sure.

SMITH: Did Dr. King talk to the crowd, address the audience?

LEWIS: I believe I heard or I am not too sure whether Dr. King spoke before the march or after the march.

SMITH: Was anything said in the church by anybody addressing the group about the march on Tuesday afternoon; was it planned there or mentioned or suggested?

LEWIS: Well, if I may say something here, I was in and out of the church, you see, you have a sanctuary, then you have an office, and many times I was passing through the sanctuary into the church, and I didn't pay that much attention to what was going on, because I had no—well, I was not going to participate in the march, myself, and—

SMITH: Did you leave the crowd of people at the church or did you follow the crowd of people on Tuesday?

LEWIS: On Tuesday during the march, I believe I remained next door in the parsonage; at that time I was feeling very bad, and I was still under a doctor's care and—like I am now, and—

SMITH: You didn't go up to the bridge?

LEWIS: I did not.

SMITH: You stayed completely out of the vicinity of the march on Tuesday; is that correct?

LEWIS: Right.

SMITH: Do you know Reverend James J. Reeb*?

LEWIS: I know Reverend Reeb; I met him for the first time.

SMITH: Did he die last evening in Birmingham?

LEWIS: From newspaper reports and from radio reports, that is what—

SMITH: Did you see him in Selma on Tuesday?

LEWIS: I remember seeing him at the church or in the parsonage, I am not sure whether it was early Tuesday morning, around noon, late Tuesday afternoon, I am not sure.

SMITH: Did he participate in the march Tuesday?

LEWIS: I am not sure whether he participated in the march; I have no way of supporting—

SMITH: Did you observe any crowd of white people in the vicinity of Brown's Chapel on Tuesday or at any other points in Selma on Tuesday at about the same time the marching or the demonstration was carried on in the street?

---

*   Reverend James Reeb was a white Unitarian Universalist minister and member of the Southern Christian Leadership Conference who participated in the march on March 7. On March 9, 1965, Reeb and three other ministers were attacked by white segregationists, and two days later he died of head injuries sustained in the attack. The murder remains officially unsolved.

LEWIS: Well, there was many white people all around on Sylvan Street and all around Brown's Chapel.

SMITH: Did they appear to be hostile?

LEWIS: I don't know, I didn't pay that much attention; I saw a lot of people, I saw priests, nuns, I really didn't pay that much attention to the people, to the face.

SMITH: Were law enforcement people there to or attempting to keep other crowds of bystanders back from the marchers?

LEWIS: I wouldn't know.

SMITH: You didn't see any of that?

LEWIS: I didn't see anyone there, didn't see no law enforcement agent.

SMITH: Did you see any state troopers there?

LEWIS: To the best of my knowledge, on Tuesday I did not; I didn't pay that much attention, because I was not personally that much involved and tried to avoid crowds as much as possible.

SMITH: Did you make a statement this morning for NBC that was televised nationally?

LEWIS: I did not make a statement this morning.

SMITH: Did you make one last evening?

LEWIS: I spoke to a group of people last evening.

SMITH: Did you make it before an NBC television camera?

LEWIS: I don't know whether NBC or CBS or ABC or any other network was around.

SMITH: Did you make it before a national television camera?

LEWIS: I made it before a group of people that was involved in a prayer vigil in memorial, in tribute to Reverend Reeb.

SMITH: Where were you when you made the statement?

LEWIS: I made it in Selma.

SMITH: Did a group of people hear this statement?

LEWIS: They was there.

SMITH: I mean present?

LEWIS: They were there in a prayerful manner, and I am sure that they heard the statement.

SMITH: How many people were there when you made the statement?

LEWIS: I don't know.

SMITH: Well, would you give us your best judgment?

LEWIS: I would say 150 or 200.

SMITH: Did you say this, or this in substance, I could be incorrect in my quotation: "This is a revolution, this is a war, a nonviolent revolution, a nonviolent war"; did you say that?

LEWIS: I did—I said that this is a revolution, that this is a war that we are engaged in, that it is a nonviolent war where people commit themselves to the philosophy of nonviolence, not simply as a technique or as a tactic, but as a philosophy or as a way of life.

SMITH: How did the crowd of people that were present when you made, when you made the statement, react to the statement that you had made?

LEWIS: Well, the people standing there, that was standing there in a prayerful manner, that was standing there with a sense of pride and at the same time with a sense of dignity and with a sense of humility.

SMITH: What is your understanding of the word, "revolution"?

HALL: Your honor please, we are going to object to this.

THE COURT: Sustain it.

SMITH: Do you know Carl Braden?*

LEWIS: I know of Mr. Braden; I have seen him around.

SMITH: Where did you last see him?

LEWIS: I would say that I do not know; it has been maybe a year or two years since I saw him last.

SMITH: Where did you last see Mr. Braden?

LEWIS: I do not know, have the slightest idea; I travel across this country, and I have been out of the country for some time; I meet many, many people, and I do not keep a tab.

SMITH: How long have you known Mr. Braden?

LEWIS: I have seen him around, I guess the past two or three years.

SMITH: I am not trying to put words in your mouth; do you know him?

LEWIS: I do not know him. I know of him, I met him; I believe the first time I met him, I met him when I was a student at Fisk University in Nashville, Tennessee.

SMITH: When was that?

* A journalist and activist most famous for the Supreme Court case *Braden v. United States.*

LEWIS: I believe that was in the fall of '61. I am not sure.

SMITH: What was the occasion for you to meet him?

HALL: Your honor please, we are going to object to all this about Carl Braden, who is not in this lawsuit.

THE COURT: I sustain objection to that question.

HALL: Thank you.

SMITH: That was at Fisk University in 1963, you say?

LEWIS: '61, I believe.

SMITH: Since you met him or knew who he was, when did you next see him, or my question is, when is the most recent time that you have seen Carl Braden?

LEWIS: I don't know or have the slightest idea, sir.

SMITH: Have you communicated with him by telephone?

LEWIS: I have no communication with him, never communicated—

SMITH: Do you know James Dombrowski?*

---

*   Cofounder of the Highlander Folk School in Monteagle, Tennessee, to train labor and civil rights activists.

LEWIS: I have seen him; I do not know him.

SMITH: Where have you seen him?

LEWIS: I am not sure; I believe the first time I met him or first time I saw him was at a memorial service or a tribute to someone in DC; I am not too sure about that.

SMITH: Have you ever attended a meeting with him or a meeting in which he was present?

LEWIS: I don't think so.

SMITH: In his lifetime did you know Malcolm X?

NORMAN AMAKER: Your honor, object to that question.

HALL: Oh, boy.

THE COURT: I will let him answer it; overrule.

LEWIS: I met the late Malcolm X.

SMITH: When did you meet him?

LEWIS: I think the first time that I met the late Malcolm X [was] just before the March on Washington, the day before the same day of the March on Washington, and I met him in passing, it was the morning of August 28, in the Statler Hilton Hotel, and I said, "Hello, Malcolm," and he said, "Hello, Mr. Lewis," or something like that.

SMITH: Since that time have you had any further contact with him, up until his death?

LEWIS: When he was abroad during the last fall, I saw him in Kenya.

SMITH: In where?

LEWIS: In Kenya, in Nairobi, Kenya, in Africa.

SMITH: Was this by coincidence that you saw him there, or was it a prearranged meeting?

LEWIS: Just coincidence; we happened to be passing through going to another country for the independence celebration, and it was coincidental that we saw Malcolm.

SMITH: Why were you in Kenya?

LEWIS: Passing through on my way to Gambia for the independence celebration.

SMITH: How long were you there?

JACK GREENBERG: Objection, your honor.

THE COURT: Sustain it.

GREENBERG: This is so diversionary.

THE COURT: Sustain it.

SMITH: What was the purpose of the mass demonstration in Selma on March 7?

LEWIS: The purpose of the mass demonstration March 7 was simply walking from Selma to Montgomery to seek the aid and assistance of Governor Wallace in granting the Negro citizens of the Black Belt of Alabama and the whole State of Alabama their constitutional right, their voting right, and to seek an end to police brutality.

SMITH: Did you have knowledge or notice of the statement or proclamation of the governor of this state made on March 6 stating in substance that, "this march cannot and will not be tolerated or permitted"?

LEWIS: On the afternoon of March 6, one of our staff members informed me when I was in Atlanta that the governor had issued an order, a ban on the demonstration.

SMITH: You knew about that on the day it was made?

LEWIS: On the afternoon of the sixth.

SMITH: Now, were you a leader of the march on the seventh, the following day?

LEWIS: I did participate, I guess, as a leader of the march on March 7.

SMITH: You disregarded the statement or proclamation of the governor?

LEWIS: Well, I felt that the order, the ban by Governor Wallace, was an unjust ban, it was an unjust order, and that we had a constitutional right to [a] peaceful march from Selma to Montgomery.

SMITH: Were you aware of the fact that the case of the *United States v. Atkins* had been pending in the Federal Court for the Southern District of Alabama for approximately five years in regard to voter registration?

LEWIS: I had some knowledge of it on March 7; I had some knowledge of it before March 7; but my knowledge of it is very vague; I do not keep up with the whole legal operation.

SMITH: Based on your knowledge or what has been told you, did discrimination of Negroes continue in the voter registration process in Dallas County after Judge Thomas issued an injunction against the Dallas County Board of Registrars?

LEWIS: Well, from the information that our office was able to receive from the Dallas County Voters League and from my own personal observation in Selma and Dallas County, I think discrimination of Negro people who were attempting to register to vote was continuing.

SMITH: Did you or did anyone else to your knowledge bring this to the attention of the court or to the Justice Department?

LEWIS: I did not, and I have no knowledge of anyone else; I couldn't really say, I don't know; but I did not.

SMITH: Isn't it a fact that one purpose of the street demonstration is to arouse Negro citizens to go down and exercise the rights which federal courts have given them in the voter registration suits?

LEWIS: I would say that one purpose of the demonstration, whether they be voter registration or demonstration to protest police brutality, is to dramatize the issue, not only to arouse the Negro people, but to dramatize that there is a problem, that people are being denied their constitutional rights, and to call attention to it.

SMITH: Do you consider these mass demonstrations to be successful whether or not violence erupts or occurs as an incident to them?

LEWIS: Well, I consider the use of nonviolent, massive

nonviolent, direct action to be successful whether the demonstration are nonviolent, because the demonstrations that we are going to engage in are going to be nonviolent.

SMITH: These demonstrations in Selma since you have been there have on numerous occasions caused acts of violence?

LEWIS: But since I have been in Selma, all of the demonstrations that I have observed have been strictly and almost totally nonviolent and peaceful.

SMITH: Nonviolent and peaceful on the part of the white community?

LEWIS: Well, what I am trying to say here, that as far as the demonstrators are concerned, the plan of demonstration is peaceful, orderly, and nonviolent, and we are saying if there is going to be violence, it will not come from those of us who be participating in the demonstration, in the march.

SMITH: What you have done or what has been done has on numerous occasions caused violence, hasn't it?

LEWIS: Well, I would say that some people had resisted our efforts to get the right to vote in Selma and Dallas County, they resisted our efforts to protest police brutality; instead, they engage in more police brutality, they beat more people, they shoot more people, and even kill more people.

SMITH: Were there any acts of violence, to your knowledge, in Selma, Alabama, or Dallas County, prior to the mass demonstrations on the streets in Selma in regard to the voter registration?

LEWIS: I don't know.

SMITH: You don't know of any?

LEWIS: I—I say I don't know.

SMITH: I have no further questions.

CROSS EXAMINATION BY MR. [W. MCLEAN] PITTS

PITTS: I will ask you one question here; you say they beat more people, they kill more people, and they shoot more people; you are talking about law enforcement officers?

LEWIS: Yes.

PITTS: In Dallas County, I believe you said?

LEWIS: Not only in Dallas County, but in the total Black Belt area where we have been involved in the past few months.

PITTS: All right; now, in Dallas County, Alabama, can you name any person that has been shot by any member of the Jim Clark['s] sheriff deputies or his posse?

LEWIS: I cannot name any person that has been shot by Sheriff Clark or some of his deputies or members of the posse.

PITTS: As a matter of fact, there has not been one person even fired at by a member of the deputies; isn't that correct?

LEWIS: Well, I do not know; but I have seen members of the posse. I saw a member of the posse on Sunday reach for his gun.

PITTS: I am talking about shooting; has a shot been fired?

LEWIS: I do not know.

PITTS: All right. So you are not—but you know of no person that has been shot by any of them—killed?

LEWIS: I do not.

THE COURT: You still restricting it to Dallas County?

PITTS: Yes, sir.

LEWIS: I do not know of any person that has been shot or killed by a member of the posse.

PITTS: All right; now, this instance that Mr. Smith asked you about this white minister, Reb—is that his name, Reb?

LEWIS: Reverend Reeb.

PITTS: Reverend Reeb; he was beat up down in the—near a Negro area of the town on Washington Street by four white men that were not law enforcement officers; isn't that correct?

LEWIS: Well, I do not know who beat him up.

PITTS: All right; and how many times have you led marches on the Dallas County Courthouse?

LEWIS: I don't know.

PITTS: Well, in your best judgment? Since January, now?

LEWIS: Oh, since January; well, I would say three or four times.

PITTS: Now, does that include the month of January?

LEWIS: Since January 18.

PITTS: Now, how many marches have been marched on the Dallas County Courthouse?

LEWIS: I do not know.

PITTS: As a matter of fact, it has been from three to five per day, hasn't it?

LEWIS: I do not know.

PITTS: All right. Now, what is the largest group of people that you got around the Dallas County Courthouse?

LEWIS: Well, I do not know the largest group, but from press report I understand that the largest group that went down was about fifteen hundred, and on that particular day I happened to be out of Selma.

PITTS: What is the second largest group?

LEWIS: I would say a thousand.

PITTS: And the smallest group?

LEWIS: The people have gone down in twos, threes, fours, and fives.

PITTS: All right. Now, that group of people, when they would be down there, wouldn't there be white people all around on the opposite side of the street, all these people would march right to the front door of the courthouse, or the Lauderdale Street door of the courthouse, wouldn't they?

LEWIS: Most of the white people that I have seen down during the demonstration have been newsmen, members of the posse, and sheriff's deputies.

PITTS: You haven't seen [a] mass of white people standing over on the corner?

LEWIS: I have seen, I have seen on occasion white people standing on the corner.

PITTS: Were you down at the Dallas County Courthouse— you knew that Judge James A. Hare had entered an order of injunction [to] prohibit demonstrations around the Dallas County Courthouse while court was in session, didn't you?

LEWIS: To the best of my knowledge, I think I was out of the city, perhaps out of the state, during the time that Judge Hare issued that order.

PITTS: Was that order ever served on you?

LEWIS: No.

PITTS: You now, you did know that the city of Selma also had a parade statute; is that right?

LEWIS: I heard that.

PITTS: Have you ever made application to the department— to the city for a parade permit?

LEWIS: As an individual I haven't, [to] the best of my knowledge, I don't know—

PITTS: Do you know of your organization making any such—

LEWIS: Well, I wouldn't know; I believe the Dallas County Voters League or other individuals or groups have made such requests.

PITTS: And you do know that Martin Luther King and a group were arrested for violating that parade ordinance, don't you?

LEWIS: I heard of that.

PITTS: Now, have you ever been engaged or did you ever send anyone down to picket the Federal Building down in Selma?

LEWIS: I never sent anyone down to the county to the Federal Building to picket the United States Courthouse.

PITTS: I—well, to carry signs around it?

LEWIS: I never sent anyone down to—

PITTS: Did your organization do that?

LEWIS: Well, I would say that some local citizens of Dallas County and Selma on one occasion, I believe in '63, stood on the Federal steps with signs saying, "One man one vote," "The Dallas County Negroes want to register and vote," and "Let my people register and vote." May I say this; as an organization we do not make decisions for local people; I do not tell people to do this and do that. We believe in group leadership the local people decide for themselves.

PITTS: But you recommend to them various procedures that they can go about to do; isn't that right? Such as toting signs and demonstrations and things like that?

LEWIS: My participation is more one of service, to be used in any way that I can be helpful in the movement.

PITTS: All right. Now, let me ask you this; how long has [the] Student Nonviolent Coordinating Committee had its office over there in the Sullivan Building in Selma? That is [the] building directly across the street from the city hall?

LEWIS: I know where the building is; I have spent some time in there. I believe our office has been there since the spring of '63.

PITTS: Is Frank Sirocco one of the workers of that Student Nonviolent Coordinating Committee?

LEWIS: Frank Sirocco been working with the Student Non-violent Coordinating Committee.

PITTS: And is Carol Lawson one of them?

LEWIS: Carol Lawson, if I recall, was down in Selma last fall working with a literacy program teaching young Negro students.

PITTS: All right. Now, who else would you name who is in Selma that is in that Student Nonviolent Coordinating Committee who are in Selma as workers who are not residents of Selma?

LEWIS: You want me to name the local—the staff members of the Student Nonviolent Coordinating Committee that are working—

PITTS: Yes, that are in there working with the Student Nonviolent who are nonresidents of the city of Selma?

LEWIS: Well, we have a few people there; we have John Love, Silus Norman, Larry Fox, Faye Bellamy, and there is maybe others sort of slipped my—

PITTS: Now, was Wolf Dawson one of them?

LEWIS: Wolf Dawson was down in September of '63, was not a staff member, not a staff worker for the Student Nonviolent Coordinating Committee.

PITTS: What about C. T. Vivian?

LEWIS: I believe C. T. Vivian is not a staff worker for Student Nonviolent Coordinating Committee.

PITTS: Who is he connected with?

LEWIS: To the best of my knowledge, he is working with the Southern Christian Leadership Conference.

PITTS: And he is connected with Martin Luther King; is that right?

LEWIS: Dr. King is president of the Southern Christian Leadership Conference.

PITTS: Now, have you been in Selma since Sunday, since the march on Sunday?

LEWIS: Yes, I have been there since Sunday.

PITTS: All right. Now, you had the march on Tuesday, didn't you?

LEWIS: I did not participate in the march on Tuesday.

PITTS: I meant you had a march there on Tuesday, one we are talking about, one that crossed the River Bridge and come back; is that right?

LEWIS: From my own observation and from press reports—

PITTS: I withdraw the question; I was just trying to get a point of time. There was a march that started out for Montgomery on Tuesday; isn't that right?

LEWIS: Yes.

PITTS: All right; now, when that march got back, was another march immediately planned for night marching there in Selma?

LEWIS: I don't know.

PITTS: Were you there? At Brown's Chapel?

LEWIS: I have been in Selma; I have been at Brown Chapel; as I said earlier, I had very little to do with any plans for any meeting since March 7.

PITTS: How many times at Brown's Chapel since Tuesday at noon?

LEWIS: I don't know; maybe two or three times.

PITTS: Is it a fact that the police have had some thousand Negroes contained in front of Brown's Chapel from early Tuesday evening, all of Tuesday night, all of yesterday?

LEWIS: Well, from what I have observed since late Tuesday, hundreds and perhaps thousands, but more or less hundreds of Negro and white people, rabbis, ministers, priests, nuns, have been force[d] to live in what I consider a police state, a tactic situation, they are surrounded by state troopers, they are surrounded by members of sheriff's posse and some of the deputies; they are forced to—in and around Brown's Chapel A.M.E. Church.

PITTS: You know that in fact the corner of Selma Street and Sylvan Street the police have contained this group in front of A.M.E. Chapel; is that correct?

LEWIS: This was the situation on Tuesday.

PITTS: All right; now, it is a fact that they won't let any white people from out in a car or any type go down there; isn't that right?

LEWIS: I don't know; I am not white, and I wouldn't know.

PITTS: Huh, and they have turned away groups after groups of white people that have been trying to go down there; isn't that correct?

LEWIS: I don't know.

PITTS: And as a matter of fact, if it had not been—I withdraw that question. As a matter of fact, the sheriff, sheriff's posse, state troopers, have been present to protect you people as you were marching down the street; isn't that correct?

LEWIS: I don't know.

PITTS: And isn't it a fact that Captain Wilson Baker, of the Selma Police Department, have advised—Have you met with him?

LEWIS: I have seen Mr. Baker on a few occasions, in and around Brown's Chapel since January 18.

PITTS: Now, you have talked with him on several occasions, now, haven't you?

LEWIS: I have seen him; I spoke with him.

PITTS: And you have talked to him about these demonstrations, haven't you?

LEWIS: Well, I have talked with Mr. Baker from time to time when I walking down the street or when I am engaged in a peaceful march.

PITTS: All right, and he has told you, he's been down there and begged you all to stop these demonstrations because he didn't know how long he was going to be able to contain a certain group of white people; isn't that right?

LEWIS: He never said that to me.

PITTS: Huh, and he was telling you all for your own protection you ought to cut this demonstrating out, didn't he?

LEWIS: He never said that to me.

PITTS: Now, how—who is in charge of the juvenile end of this movement that you speak about?

LEWIS: What? In this movement it is a mass movement, and it is no such thing as discriminating people individually. It is a people movement, and whether people be young or whether they be—

PITTS: Your honor, I ask him to answer my question.

THE COURT: As to who was in charge of the juvenile part of the movement?

LEWIS: No one in particular in charge of juveniles; we have no juvenile division in the movement.

PITTS: Do you know that they have been staying out of school?

LEWIS: I have heard of reports that people have been staying out of school. I have been at the church on school days, and I have seen people stay out of school.

PITTS: And do you know that out of Hudson High School, approximately fifteen hundred students, there would have been thirteen—over a thousand absences in one day at that school?

LEWIS: I have heard of that; I do not know it.

PITTS: And do you know that has been continuous since January?

LEWIS: I do not know that.

PITTS: And have you been told that the courts in Selma and police authorities have been trying to get these children to go back to school?

LEWIS: I do not know of that.

PITTS: All right. Has the Student Nonviolent Coordinating Committee been active in any boycotting in Selma?

LEWIS: The Student Nonviolent Coordinating Committee's only function in Selma is more or less of a service function. From what I gather, the Negro people of Dallas County, the Negro people of Selma, decided that they would have an economic withdrawal. The people made that decision; the Student Nonviolent Coordinating Committee did not make that decision.

PITTS: Well, do you know of any active boycott that is going on in Selma now, the Selma Bus Lines?

LEWIS: I have heard that people are not riding the Selma Bus Lines.

PITTS: And they were encouraged not to ride it, wasn't they, in mass meeting, wasn't they told not to ride it?

LEWIS: To the best of my knowledge, I have not been in a mass meeting where I have heard this.

PITTS: Well, do you know—let me ask you this; do you know of any group of squads that have gone down to the bus stations and threatened people that were getting [on] those busses?

LEWIS: I have no knowledge of anything of this nature …

PITTS: And did you know that the people were having to protect those busses as they went along the route because of these squads that were threatening people?

LEWIS: I have no knowledge of anything—This is my first time hearing anything like this.

PITTS: I'll ask you this, did the Student Nonviolent Coordinating Committee purchase or furnish the funds for the purchase of three Volkswagens?

NORMAN AMAKER: Your honor, excuse me; if Mr. Pitts wants to testify, I suggest he be sworn.

PITTS: I asked him did he know it.

THE COURT: The testimony is the evidence; do you know the answer?

LEWIS: I wouldn't know that. The Student Nonviolent

Coordinating Committee is rather a poor, poor organization; we can't afford to buy three Volkswagens.

THE COURT: Did you purchase those busses?

LEWIS: We did not.

PITTS: You know about those busses, though, didn't you?

LEWIS: I have no knowledge of the busses.

REDIRECT EXAMINATION BY MR. [PETER A.] HALL

HALL: Mr. Lewis, I would like to direct your attention to the demonstration in 1963 which you have testified about on cross examination, I believe, where there were persons walking around the Federal Building and the county courthouse in Selma; I ask you if you were there on that occasion, were you not; you did say so on cross examination; is that right?

LEWIS: Right.

HALL: At that time and on that occasion, were there persons placed on the Federal property with signs?

LEWIS: Young people took position on the steps of the Federal Building.

HALL: And what did they do, just stand there on the steps?

LEWIS: They stood with signs; some of their signs read, "One man one vote," others read, "Let my people vote," "Dallas County Negro citizens want to register and vote."

HALL: Were they requested to leave these premises by the federal authorities or anyone else?

LEWIS: I have no knowledge of any federal officials or federal authority requesting them to leave.

HALL: Were they arrested there?

LEWIS: They were arrested and jailed by Sheriff Jim Clark and members of his deputies.

HALL: And this was a voter registration demonstration?

LEWIS: It was a voter registration demonstration.

HALL: Mr. Lewis, has most of the demonstrations since January, 1965, been on behalf of voter registration?

LEWIS: Most of the demonstrations, I would say 90 percent or 95 percent of all the demonstrations in Dallas County and Selma have been voter registration demonstrations.

HALL: There have been some—

LEWIS: Some demonstrations have been demonstrations to protest police brutality.

HALL: So all of the demonstrations have been concerned with either voter registration or to protest police brutality?

LEWIS: Right.

HALL: And when you say, "police brutality," what police brutality was involved?

LEWIS: Well, on numerous occasions.

THE COURT: You mean what agency?

HALL: Yes, sir; what agency?

LEWIS: The Sheriff's Department, Sheriff Clark, some of the deputies, and members of the posse.

HALL: I'll ask you, Mr. Lewis, to tell us if it isn't—if you know whether or not it is a fact that most of the persons who have been in lines of march to the Dallas County Courthouse since January, 1965, have been persons who were attempting to either register and vote or to sign the appearance—

PITTS: We object to that question; it has been no voting days, your honor.

THE COURT: Answer it to the extent of your knowledge; objection is overruled.

LEWIS: To the best of my knowledge, most of the people

have been involved in the marches, in the demonstration, to the Dallas County Courthouse have been local citizens of Dallas County over twenty-one [who] were trying to register and vote.

HALL: That's all; thank you.

RECROSS EXAMINATION BY MR. [MAURY D.] SMITH

SMITH: Were the demonstrations in September of 1963 that were conducted in or near the Federal Building in Selma for the purpose of influencing the federal court that had jurisdiction of voter registration case[s] there?

LEWIS: The demonstration that was held on the step of the Federal Building in September of '63 was not for the purpose of forcing the federal court. Many people have been arrested days before that demonstration at the Dallas County Courthouse carrying signs saying, "One man one vote." Some of the people decided to demonstrate on the step of the Federal Building to make a witness, to dramatize that people in Dallas County, in Selma, Negro people, [are] denied the right to register and vote.

SMITH: Did you know at that time that Judge Daniel Thomas had within the jurisdiction of his court the voter registration matter involving the Board of Registrars of Dallas County?

LEWIS: I am not sure.

SMITH: Were you on the steps of the Federal Building?

LEWIS: I was not on the steps of the Federal Building.

SMITH: Were you there in the vicinity of the Federal Building?

SMITH: I was in the vicinity of the Federal Building.

SMITH: How near the Federal Building were you?

LEWIS: If I recall, I was standing down the street about almost a block from the Federal Building.

SMITH: As a member or the National Director of the Student Nonviolent Coordinating Committee, have you been given instructions by anyone as to how to plan and conduct mass demonstrations of citizens?

SMITH: No, I haven't been given any instructions how to plan mass demonstrations of Negro citizens.

SMITH: None whatsoever?

LEWIS: None whatsoever.

RECROSS EXAMINATION BY MR. PITTS

PITTS: You were familiar and you knew about the decree of injunction or order of Judge Thomas, United States judge, that specified that a book was to be put out in [the] front door of the courthouse, and the Lauderdale Street entrance was to be used, and persons desiring to register was to sign that book and get a number; were you familiar with that?

LEWIS: I have some vague knowledge of that order or decree by Judge Thomas.

PITTS: And Judge Thomas laid down how they were to get in line to register to vote; is that right? I mean to register; is that right?

LEWIS: I am not too sure about the specific of the order; I believe as much as possible the people who had been involved in the demonstration have tried to follow that line of decree by the judge.

PITTS: Now, since the judge entered that order, and since the people have been signing that book, you all have been continuously marching to that courthouse, haven't you?

LEWIS: To the best of my knowledge, since that order we have been bringing or suggesting that hundreds and hundreds of Negroes go down to carry out the court order to attempt to register to vote, to sign the book, and I believe since that order more [than] twenty-two hundred people have signed the book.

PITTS: And—but you have still continued these demonstrations [on] the streets of the City of Selma, haven't you?

LEWIS: All the demonstrations, or most of demonstrations, I believe all of the demonstrations, not including the demonstration on March 7, have been directed toward the Dallas County Courthouse for the purpose of signing that book.

PITTS: But you have continued those demonstrations after this book was put out there and this procedure was worked out, haven't you?

LEWIS: We have continued to march down to the county courthouse to attempt to register to vote.

PITTS: Now, you say, "we"; who is "we"?

LEWIS: The Negro citizens of Dallas County have gone down with some other citizens to sign the book, to wait, to not to give up.

PITTS: But you have also these march, this march to Montgomery on Sunday and the other marches were all after that book was put out there, wasn't it; Judge Thomas entered that order, wasn't it?

LEWIS: Yes.

REDIRECT EXAMINATION BY MR. HALL

HALL: Mr. Lewis, where is the office of the Board of Registrars of Dallas County located; in what building?

LEWIS: The Board of Registrars' office is located in the Dallas County Courthouse in Selma, Alabama.

HALL: In the Dallas County Courthouse; this is where people are supposed to go to register to vote?

LEWIS: That is where people go and attempt to register to vote.

HALL: And the book which has been referred to on several occasions where the prospective registrants are to sign is located in the courthouse?

LEWIS: The book, the appearance book, is located in the Dallas County Courthouse.

HALL: Excuse me, please. Mr. Lewis, do you know whether or not Judge Thomas's order placing the book there at the courthouse for prospective registrants to sign specified that the book was to be there every day?

LEWIS: I am not sure, but to the best of my knowledge I believe it is in that order that the book is to be available for prospective registered voters every day.

AMAKER: Your honor, any objection to excusing this witness, Mr. Lewis?

PITTS: No, sir; he can go.

SMITH: I object to excusing him, excuse me; I am not at this time prepared or cannot agree to excuse him, because he is a party; I will if something develops later that I can, but at this time I would not agree to excuse a party.

JOHN DOAR: Can he be excused until Monday?

THE COURT: Are you agreeing not to excuse him solely because he is a party?

SMITH: Your honor, there is a possibility of further cross examination of him.

THE COURT: All right, then, he will remain.

"I SAW ALL AROUND ME THE SYSTEM OF SEGREGATION AND RACIAL DISCRIMINATION"

INTERVIEW BY HENRY HAMPTON
AMERICA, THEY LOVED YOU MADLY,
A PRECURSOR TO EYES ON THE PRIZE:
AMERICA'S CIVIL RIGHTS YEARS (1954-1965)
MAY 14, 1979

HENRY HAMPTON: So, where are you from and how did you get involved in the civil rights movement?

LEWIS: I grew up in rural Alabama about fifty miles south of Montgomery and the third child in a family of ten. The little place where I grew up is so small it's very difficult to locate it on the map, on the Alabama map. Martin Luther King Jr. used to refer to this place as being Four Corners, Alabama. It's near a little place called Troy. My father was a sharecropper and later, I was four years old in 1944, he had saved something like three hundred dollars, and with those three hundred dollars we moved from the plantation, and he bought a hundred and ten acres of land where my family was able to raise cotton, corn, peanuts, chickens. So it's part of my growing up permanently in rural Alabama.

HAMPTON: How did you get involved in civil rights activity?

LEWIS: Well, as a young child growing up in rural Alabama, I saw the system of segregation and racial discrimination. We had to attend school in a one-room church from the first through the sixth grade, and we had the books that were handed down from white students by the county.

Well, as I was growing up in, in rural Alabama, I saw all around me the system of segregation and racial discrimination. The visible signs in the little town of Troy, the population of about seven thousand, we saw the sign that said COLORED ONLY, WHITE ONLY, COLORED WAITING, WATER FOUNTAIN. In a little five-and-ten store was a civil fountain, a clean fountain for white people to come and drink water, but in another corner of the store there was a little spigot, a rusty spigot said COLORED DRINKING. And I became resentful of the signs and all the visible evidence of segregation and racial discrimination. My father and my uncles and my grandfather and great-grandfathers on my mother's side and my father's side, all of my relatives, have I listened to their discussions about what had happened to them.

And so, I grew up in that environment where I had to face and live with the system every day, and I don't think I had much of a choice, but to, but to resent it. And I grew up with a feeling that I had to find a way to oppose this system of segregation, racial discrimination. And my responsibility on the farm was to raise the chickens. We had a lot of chickens. And I grew up with this idea, somehow, I don't know where it came from, I wanted to, to be a minister and, somehow, I transferred my desire to be a minister and my responsibility of raising the chickens, somehow, it got together. And I literally started preaching to the chickens. They became members of this sort of invisible church or maybe you want to call it a real church. And I tried out some ideas on the, on the chickens. Later I tested same ideas on my younger brothers or sisters and first cousins. And I remember my first act of, maybe, a nonviolent protest was when my parents would kill the chicken, and I would refuse to eat the chicken, and it went for two or three days refusing to speak to my mother, father, because they killed a chicken. I thought that it was so wrong. And the one thing I did as a young child, when I was about five or six years old, I wanted to save the soul of a chicken and baptize this particular chicken and the chicken drown, and in the process of trying to save this chicken, you know, I lost the chicken. But as, I guess, my sort of childhood way of dealing with protest and getting involved in later the civil rights movement.

I was fifteen years old in the tenth grade in 1955 when I first heard of the Montgomery bus boycott. Now Montgomery is only fifty miles from where I grew up. And I heard about Martin Luther King because he came on a local radio station from Montgomery, and he was preaching sermons like most Black Baptist ministers, but I heard of this man and the sermons, eloquent. But one sermon he had was very special one Sunday morning at eleven o'clock on this radio station. It was something called Paul's message to the church at Corinth. But he took this sermon around and made it something like, Paul letter or Paul's message to the Christians of America. And he kept preaching about—he was not concerned about the streets of heaven and the pearly gates and the streets paved with milk and honey. He was more concerned about the streets of Montgomery and the way that Black people and poor people were being treated in Montgomery. And this was before December 1955 when the Montgomery bus boycott occurred. And I think, listen to

Martin Luther King Jr., and listen to my grandmother and grandfather about some of the things that had happened to them became messages, became the necessary ingredients to encourage me to identify with whatever movement or organization or cause that would rock the, the whole system of segregation and racial discrimination.

We were bussed to school after I left the sixth grade. We rode in old broken-down buses that white children had used. We didn't have any new buses. And the roads, even the roads in the Black community, where Black people owned land, were unpaved. They were left literally, deliberately, unpaved. Even skip places on—in the road. And during the winter months we would run in ditches on the way to school, because of the rain, the red mud, and the clay in that part of Alabama. And during evenings, returning from school, we would be late returning home because the bus would break down, we'd get stuck in the mud, and that type of thing. So all of these things came together and by the time I went away to college in 1957 and I was away from home and the Montgomery bus boycott had occurred in Montgomery, where we had witnessed and I saw it on television, I read about it in the newspaper—we didn't even have a subscription as a matter of fact, 'cause we were too poor, I guess, to the local daily newspaper, something called the *Montgomery Advertiser*. But my grandfather had a subscription to that paper and each day after he read the paper we would get the paper and we kept up with what was happening in Montgomery. And we listened to the radio and, and what happened in Montgomery, to watch fifty thousand Black people walk the streets for over a year rather than ride segregated buses became a source of inspiration. It, it created a sense of hope, a sense of optimism. And by going to school in Nashville, Tennessee, many, many miles away from my parents and from rural Alabama, I was—I felt freer to find a way to, to get involved. And one of the first thing I did, I became a member of the youth chapter of the NAACP in Nashville. As a matter of fact, I tried to organize a campus chapter on the campus of the American Baptist Theological Seminary, where I was a student. We didn't succeed in that effort because this little school was gently supported by the Southern Baptist Convention, which was, for the most part during that period, was all white and the National Baptist Convention. And the president of the school said we couldn't organize a chapter there, but I continued to be involved in the, in the local chapter.

HAMPTON: How did, how did, how did you get involved in the, in the sit-ins in Nashville?

LEWIS: Well—

HAMPTON: And how did, how did those sit-ins start in Nashville?

LEWIS: During the school year of '59/'60—well, even before then, there was a group of students in Nashville who had attended a, a summer workshop at Harlem Folk School, outside of Nashville and looked—

HAMPTON: So what you're saying is that you were prepared for the sit-ins?

LEWIS: Yes. I think we were prepared in, in Nashville. Nashville, at the time, was considered a sort of the citadel of education in the, in the South with all of the colleges and all of the universities there and many, many churches. Sort of progressive and liberal. There was a very active social action committee at one of the local Black Baptist churches. And at the same time, the pastor of this church, the Reverend Kelly Miller Smith, was the local president of the Nashville Christian Leadership Council, an arm of the Southern Christian Leadership Conference—had an effort going. So every Tuesday night for an entire semester in 1959 we had what we call nonviolent workshop, direct action workshop, where we discussed and debated the theory, the philosophy of Gandhi. The teaching of Gandhi. The whole question of civil disobedience. The whole history of the struggle in India and the attempt on the part of Gandhi to bring about some resolution of the problems in, in South Africa.

But the point came, rather I guess, halfway through the workshop in late November and early December of '59, to have a few test sit-in[s]. So we organized a delegation of, of young people, primarily students: white students, Black students, international students from, primarily, from Africa and from some of the Latin American country [*sic*]. We went down to two of the large department stores and occupied the lunch counter seats, went into restaurants, occupied seats at tables, and we were told that we could not be served because there were Blacks in the group. This established a case that the city of Nashville was segregated, that they refused to serve Black people. We continued the, the workshop, but when we returned during the early part of 1960, we did receive a call from a young minister by the name of Douglas Moore, this was after the Greensboro sit-ins of February 1, 1960, saying, "What can the students in Nashville do to support the students of North Carolina?" And, I guess, that was the message. That was the question that we needed, and we were ready. We had—ready to be involved, to organize mass sit-ins or sit-down demonstration in Nashville. So in a matter of two or three days, we organized, during the month of February, what we call "T" days and Saturday, a sit-in. On most of the college campuses in, in Nashville, Tuesdays and Thursdays were light days for classes, and Saturday, for the most part, was a free day. We had on that first day over five hundred student[s] together in front of Fisk University chapel, to be transported downtown to the First Baptist Church, to be organized into small groups to go down to sit in at the lunch counters. We went into the local stores for the most part. The five-and-ten, Woolworth, Kreske's, McClellan's, these stores were known all across the South, and, for the most part, all across the country. We took our seats in a very orderly, peaceful fashion. The students were dressed like they were on the way to, to church or going to a big social affair. But they had their books, and we stayed there at the lunch counter studying and preparing our homework, because we were denied service. The manager ordered that the lunch counters be closed, that the restaurants be closed, and we'd just sit there, and we continued to sit all day long.

The first day, nothing, in term of violence or any disorder, nothing happened. This continued for a few more days, and it continued day in and day out. And, finally, on one Saturday, when we had about a hundred students prepare to go down, it was a very beautiful day in Nashville, very beautiful day, we got a call from a local white minister who had been a real supporter of the movement. He said that if we go down on this particular day, he understand[s] that the police would stand to the side and let a group of white hoodlums and thugs come in and beat people up and then we would be arrested. And we should make a decision of whether we wanted to go or not, and some people tried to discourage us from going on that particular Saturday. We made a decision to go, and we all went to the same store. It was Woolworth in downtown Nashville, in the heart of the downtown area, and occupied every seat at the lunch counter, every seat in the restaurant, and it did happen. A group of young white men came in and they start pulling and, and beating, primarily the young women. Putting lighted cigarettes down their backs, in their hair, and really beating people, and in a short time, police officials came in and placed all of us under arrest, and not a single member of the white group, the people that were opposing our sit-in down at the lunch counter, were arrested. We all left out of that store singing, "We Shall Overcome." This was the first arrest in the, in the Nashville sit-in. It was the first mass arrest, I think, anyplace in the South. I believe it was February the 27th, 1960. And—

HAMPTON: Was that the first time you were arrested?

LEWIS: Was the first time that I was arrested, and growing up in the rural South it was not the thing to do, not to go to jail. It was a, it would bring shame and disgrace on the family. But for me, I tell you, it was like being involved in a holy crusade. It was, became, a badge of, of honor. I felt good about it. And I think it was in keeping with what we had been taught in the workshops, so I felt very good in, in a sense of righteous indignation about being arrested but at the same time the commitment and dedication on the part of the students.

HAMPTON: Ummm, maybe you can tell me about the day that Alexander Looby's house was bombed.

LEWIS: Well, it was early one morning, about six o'clock. Z. Alexander Looby, who had been a strong supporter and defender of civil rights, a member of the city council, the first Black member of the city council in the city of Nashville, was a NAACP Legal Defense Fund lawyer and had been the legal counsel for all of the students that had participated in the sit-in, had brought some of the original school desegregation cases, had worked with Thurgood Marshall. We heard that his house had been bombed, and all across the city on the different college campuses, we had a similar reaction, to call a meeting of the Nashville Central Committee. The Central Committee was the executive committee of the Nashville student nonviolent movement. By—I would say between six-thirty and seven o'clock—we were meeting. Shortly after seven, we had sent the mayor a, a telegram, saying to the mayor that we would have a march on city hall, and the mayor was Ben West, was the mayor's name, to protest the bombing of attorney Looby's house.

By noon we had more than five thousand students from Tennessee State, Fisk University, American Baptist

Theological Seminary, Meharry, and Vanderbilt, and people from the community with a sense of righteous indignation. It was not a noisy march. It was very orderly and people marched in twos. It was a long march, but it was, was one of the most beautiful effort on the part of the, the student community and the people of Nashville to say to the mayor, say to the business community, that we wanted to protest the bombing, but we wanted to see the City of Nashville become a desegregated city, an open city. And I'll never forget that day when we met at, at city hall. Diane Nash, as the chairperson of the Nashville student movement, met the mayor when he walked out to greet all of us. And she said something like, "Mr. Mayor, do you favor desegregation of the lunch counters?" And he said something like, "Yes, yes, young lady. I favor desegregation of the lunch counter. It's left up to the businessmen." And the *Nashville Tennessean*, which is, I guess, a progressive, moderate newspaper in, in Nashville in, in the South, carried a banner headline the next day saying something to the effect, "Mayor Favors Desegregation of the Lunch Counters." And from that day on, it was down road, I guess you, if it, it was an easy task for us to, to negotiate with the merchants, with the chamber of commerce to end segregation at all of the lunch counters, in drugstores and variety stores, the five-and-ten, and most of the restaurants in downtown Nashville. But it was not—

HAMPTON: So was it, was it a natural thing, then, for you to get involved in the Freedom Rides?

LEWIS: Yeah, it—I think it was natural. It, it was part of—it was natural for me, personally, because I had traveled almost, well, almost three-and-a-half years from Alabama, from southeast Alabama through Montgomery, through Birmingham, through—to Nashville, to attend school, by bus. And I had seen the sign saying WHITE ONLY, COLORED ONLY, WAITING.

In Troy we didn't have a bus station, but we had an area where colored people, where they had, where colored people were supposed to wait, where they had colored waiting that people, Black people, had to stand in a line saying COLORED WAITING to buy a ticket, and then come back around and get in at the front of the bus and go to the back of the bus. That was on the Greyhound bus. So the Freedom Ride was an attempt to end segregation, to end racial discrimination on the buses throughout the South. It was CORE, the Congress of Racial Equality, that had issued a call for the Freedom Ride, and I was one of the [people], as a member of the Nashville student movement, to volunteer to become a participant on the Freedom Ride. And I remember very well, this was my, well, early spring of 1961, but in the meantime we were involved in another effort in Nashville to desegregate the lunch counters—not the lunch counter, but the theaters.

See, all of the theaters in Nashville were segregated, still segregated in, in '61. We had thirteen standing-in, thirteen consecutive days of standing-in, where we literally stood in, kept other people, kept white people from going into the theater because Black people had to buy their ticket in a separate window, go in a separate door, and go upstairs and sit in something we refer to as "the buzzard roost." We couldn't sit on the main floor. So we had these standing-in, and after thirteen days of standing-in, these—the theaters in Nashville desegregated. But while that was all going on, while the standing-in was taking place, there was this appeal to go on the Freedom Ride. And I believe the Freedom Rides started in the first week in May 1961, in Washington, DC. As a matter of fact, on the night of May 3, 1961, this group of thirteen Freedom Rider [sic]—seven whites and six Black—had a dinner at a Chinese restaurant in Washington, DC. It was my first time having Chinese food, you know, for someone growing up in the South and going to school in Nashville, never had Chinese food. But we had attended a few days of workshops, had some discussion with then attorney general Robert Kennedy. We met at something called the Fellowship House in Washington.

And this meal was like the, to me, it was like the Last Supper because you didn't know what to expect going on the Freedom Ride. We had been told to expect same things in parts of Georgia, same things in parts of Alabama, in Mississippi, in Louisiana. And I remember getting on a bus coming to Washington, I guess by plane, and getting on, on the bus at the Greyhound bus station in Washington, DC, on May 4, and for my seat mate was an elderly white gentleman named Abbot Bigelow. Abbot Bigelow was from Cos Cob, Connecticut. He was a pacifist. He had been the skipper on a little ship called the *Golden Rule* out in the South Pacific protesting against the testing atomic bomb. He was a very committed guy to the philosophy and, and the discipline of nonviolent [sic]. So we got on this ride through the South. And we went in to parts of Virginia, to Lynchburg, Petersburg, and other places and without any problems. And through North Carolina, one of the riders attempted to get a shoeshine and a haircut in a so-called white barbershop in Charlotte, North Carolina. He was arrested and went to court the next day, and the judge threw the case out. We went on to Rock Hill, South Carolina, and Abbot Bigelow and myself got off the bus and we started in a so-called white waiting room. The doors of the waiting room was marked WHITE WAITING. And we started in the door, and we were met by a group of white young men that beat us and hit us, knocked us out, left us lying on the sidewalk there in front of the entrance to the, the waiting room. And, in a matter of a few minutes, a group of Rock Hill police officials came up and wanted to know whether we wanted, wanted to press charges and we said no.

I left a ride the next day, and I had to fly to Philadelphia for an interview with the American Friends Service Committee 'cause I had applied to go abroad as a, a volunteer in an international program in what then was Tanganyika, Tanzania now, and I had planned to rejoin the ride in Birmingham on Mother's Day. I don't remember the date, but it was the second Sunday in May. But the riders never really made it to Birmingham because one of the bus that I would have been on, after it made it through Georgia, it arrived in Anniston, Alabama, and on the outside of Anniston, Alabama, this bus was burned. The tires were deflated and the riders were beaten and other riders that made it to Birmingham on a Trailway bus were beaten there in Birmingham. And so, I went back to Nashville, and CORE decided to drop the Freedom Ride, to end the ride in, in Birmingham. And it was Bobby Kennedy, as the attorney general of the United States, who said that there should be a cooling-off period and the rides shouldn't continue. Those of us in Nashville, as, as a student from Nashville who had been a participant in the early ride, felt that the ride should continue.

HAMPTON: What happened in Anniston?

LEWIS: In Anniston, Alabama, the Greyhound bus carried a group of the Freedom Riders was burned. The tires was deflated and the bus just couldn't, couldn't roll, and hoodlums, members of the Klan, came on the bus, pulling people out, beating people, and all of the people had to leave the burning bus, and people were left lying on the highway from being beaten by members of the Klan. And in Birmingham, when the Trailway group arrived, they were beaten, and one gentleman needed something like fifty-three stitches to close up the wound on his head from the beating that occurred there. After the Birmingham incident, Senator, well then attorney general Robert Kennedy, said there must be a cooling-off period. And he tried to discourage any more so-called Freedom Rides into the South.

Well, as one of the participant in the original effort and as someone who had been involved in the Nashville student movement, I felt, and others felt, that the rides should continue. We got the necessary resources to continue the ride from Nashville. We went from Nashville to, to Birmingham, and outside of Birmingham, two other riders that were sitting near the front of the bus, I think on maybe the, the very first seat behind the bus driver, were arrested and taken to jail.

The other riders, we were taken into the city and later into a waiting room, and later the Commissioner of Public Safety Bull Connor told us, at least, informed us that we were being taken to jail. We were not being arrested, but we were being placed in protective custody for our own safety, for our own well-being. We went to jail that Wednesday night, May 17, 1961. We stayed in jail Thursday night. We went on a hunger strike, a fast. We refused to eat anything, refused to drink any water. And early Friday morning, I would say about two o'clock Friday morning, Bull Connor, several members of the Birmingham police force, came to our cell, took us out of the jail, and said, in effect, that they were taking us back to the college campuses in Nashville. And we got in the car. We didn't go in a, in a voluntary way. We went limp, so they literally picked us up and put us in the car, and we started back up the highway to—toward the Tennessee state line. It was about one hundred and twenty miles from Birmingham and maybe about the same distance from, from Nashville—that they literally dropped us out on the highway near a railroad crossing and said—a bus will be coming along or a train will be coming along and you can make your way back to the city of Nashville. We were frightened. We didn't know anyone in out more [sic] Alabama or out more Tennessee and we went across the railroad tracks with our baggage and came upon the house of an elderly Black couple. They had to be, at least, seventies, in their early seventies. And they were afraid to let us in, but they did. And they—when daylight came, the man went and bought food from several different places because he didn't want to indicate in any way that he had some unwanted guests in this small town. And the people had heard on the radio about the Freedom Riders from Nashville going to Birmingham.

In the meantime, we made a telephone call to the head-quarters of the Nashville student movement and spoke to Diane Nash, who was the leader of the effort there, and told her what had happened. And she said, "What do you want to do? Do you want to come back to Nashville or do you want to go back to Birmingham and continue the ride?" And we told her that we wanted to continue the ride. She sent a car to pick us up, and she informed us that ten other packages had been shipped by other means. She was suggesting or telling us through a code that ten other Freedom Riders had left by train to join us in Birmingham. See, the people in Nashville and around the country thought we were still in jail. And other people were going to come to Birmingham and go from Birmingham to continue the ride. We got in this car. When the car arrived, seven of us and the driver got back to Birmingham and met with Fred Shuttlesworth and some lo-cal people and student, particularly one student, Ruby Doris Smith, who made it from Atlanta and Spelman College to join the ride. And we attempted to get on the bus about five-thirty p.m., and this bus driver said, "I cannot—I will not drive." And he said something like, I will never forget what this bus driver said, he said, "I have only one life to give." It was a classic statement. "I have only one life to give, and I'm not going to give it to the NAACP, not to CORE." This was a white bus driver in Birmingham, Alabama. Didn't have any Black bus drivers at that time.

In the meantime, we understood from some of the reporters that Robert Kennedy was negotiating with the officials of Greyhound to get the bus, at least, to get us out of Birmingham during that night. And Robert Kennedy kept asking Greyhound officials, did they have any, then, Negro bus drivers, and they kept saying no. We tried at eight-thirty, throughout the night, to get a bus and we, we didn't get a bus. No bus driver would drive because the bus drivers were literally afraid of what could happen, because the Klan had surrounded the, the bus station. They were throwing stink bomb. There were police officials there trying to keep the Klan from getting to us inside of this so-called white waiting room. They had the police dogs. But it was not until eight-thirty Saturday morning, May 21st, that we understood that an arrangement had been worked out where—between the Justice Department and the officials of Greyhound and the officials of the state of Alabama—where we would board the bus with other customers or passengers and there would be two officials of Greyhound. A private plane would fly over the bus, there would be a state patrol car every fifteen or twenty miles along the highway between Birmingham and Montgomery, about ninety miles. We got on the bus and a great many of the riders really, literally, took a nap. They went to sleep. I took a seat on the front seat right behind the driver with a young man by the name of Jim Spur, a young white guy. I was a spokesman for this particular group of riders, and we did see the plane.

But I would say about forty miles or less from the city of Montgomery, all sign of protection disappeared. There was no plane, no patrol car, and when we arrived at the bus station it was just like eerie, just a strange feeling. It was so quiet, so peaceful, nothing. And the moment, literally, the moment we started down the steps off of that bus, an angry mob, they grew into about two to three thousand people, came out of nowhere: men, women, children with baseball bats, clubs, chains, and they literally—there was no police official around—they just started beating people. And we tried to get all of the women on the ride into a taxicab. There was one cab there, and this driver said he couldn't, he couldn't take the group because it was an interracial group. We had Black and white women in this particular group. And one of the Freedom Riders, was a young Black female student, said something like, "Well, I will drive myself. I will drive the cab." And the driver said no, but finally, the driver did drive off with all of the Black women, and the white women start running down the street, and then the mob literally turned on the media, on members of the press. There was one cameraman, I believe from NBC, had one of these heavy old pieces of camera equipment on his shoulder. This member of the mob took this equipment, bashed this guy, literally knocked him down, bashed his face in. So they beat up all of the reporters. Then they turned on the, the Black male members and, and white male members of, of the group. I was beaten. I think I was hit with a, a sort of crate thing that hold soda bottles and left lying in the street unconscious there in the streets of Montgomery. And I, I literally thought it was the last march. It was the last Freedom Ride. It was a, it was a very bloody event. It was a very nasty mob. There were other people that was beaten. An aide to President Kennedy who tried to intervene or get between the—

HAMPTON: How did people get away that night?

LEWIS: Well, after the dust settled from, from the violence that had occurred in, in Montgomery there was no—

HAMPTON: Why didn't you want to talk to the FBI?

LEWIS: Well, we had some real reservations about communicating with the FBI. We had heard in—from, really, from what I had seen, that for the most part, they spent most of their time taking pictures, taking notes, and we felt that they were somehow part of the local police establishment, that they were friends of the local police chief, of the police commissioner, the public safety commissioner, and we didn't trust the local FBI. Most of the FBI agents in Montgomery, on that particular day, apparently, were from Birmingham, Mobile, and other parts of the South. And we had received a, a suggestion from, I guess, John Doar, who then was the assistant attorney general in charge of civil rights, and he had suggested to us that we shouldn't talk to anyone before we were interviewed by him.

HAMPTON: Was—there was an early planning session with— that Bayard Rustin and A. Philip Randolph called in planning the March on Washington—of just activist groups. Could you tell me why was it just activist groups and, and just tell me that the conference happened and why was it just activist groups?

LEWIS: Well, Bayard Rustin and A. Philip Randolph called together the leadership, I guess, of the, of the civil rights

movement, primarily SNCC, CORE, and the representative of SCLC. In the early, early days, this was after Birmingham, this was after the mass arrests at jail and the fire
hoses and the beating in Birmingham, this was after Med-
gar Evers has been shot and two young people had enrolled
at the University of Alabama. And there was some problem
with going to the NAACP or to the Urban League, but—

HAMPTON: What was the problem?

LEWIS: Well, SNCC, the Student Nonviolent Coordinating
Committee; CORE, the Congress of Racial Equality; and
the Southern Christian Leadership Conference and, I think,
Bayard Rustin and Mr. Randolph, I think we represented
something somewhat different. We represented a, more of
a mass movement. The NAACP had played a tremendous
role in the movement. Played a superb role, but it had a long
history of taking most of the efforts to the courts, and they
were not really ready, in my estimation, to support a mass
march. Some of the people felt that it would be embarrassing
to the Kennedy Administration and were very cautious about
identifying with any idea of having a march on Washington.
I remember the first meeting that we had in Washington in,
in June of 1963 with President Kennedy. Was at that meeting that Mr. Randolph said something like, "Mr. President,
the masses are restless and we're gonna march. We're gonna
march on Washington." President Kennedy didn't understand that and he was a little frightened by it and he was
troubled. And, I think, some of the other participants, some

of the other leaders there that represented, say, the Urban League, the NACP [*sic*], and one or two of the officials of the administration, didn't understand what Mr. Randolph was saying. But he said it and, and, and restated the case like only A. Phillip Randolph could do and he did it well. He was highly and well respected, I think, particularly by this—the people in SNCC, the people in CORE, and, and the people in SCLC, because of his early leadership as a, you know, he was looked upon as a, as a militant, as a radical of a, of another period. In spite of his age, he was very young and ready to go and demand all of the things that Black people needed and wanted at that time.

HAMPTON: Who paid the bills for the March on Washington?

LEWIS: Well, I would say a different organizations, different community people throughout the country raised money. But first of all, you had to get certain people to buy into, to the, to supporting the march. Little thing happened, one story that the people probably never know. In a, in a meeting in July, the first meeting, July 1963 at the Roosevelt Hotel in New York, a leader meeting took place on July 2nd, 1963. There were some people didn't want Bayard Rustin as the director, some Black people, some Black leaders. They thought he was too radical, he was too militant, he had been identified with the left. And there was one leader of the NAACP and a leader of the Urban League insisted that Mr. Randolph ask Mr. Rustin to leave the meeting. And, at one point, Mr. Randolph had to ask Bayard Rustin to leave the meeting because of the insistence on the part of Mr. Wilkin [*sic*], on the part of Whitney Young. Fred Shuttlesworth, and Reverend Abernathy was asked to leave. James Foreman of, of SNCC was asked to leave, and Mr. Wilkins kept insisting that only the head of the organization, but for a period Mr. Wilkin [*sic*] had today—and it's not to say anything bad about the man— but he had a problem dealing with young people. He had a problem dealing with people that didn't share his ideas. But in the end, Mr. Randolph carried the day, because we suggested in that meeting, in that discussion, particularly James Farmer, Martin King, and myself, that Mr. Randolph be the chairperson of the March on Washington and that he be free to select the person of, of his choice to be the director, to be the deputy director, whatever, and he selected Bayard Rustin to direct the march.

HAMPTON: Were there any white folks involved in the planning of the march?

LEWIS: Not until, till later, when—you had here the traditional civil rights organizations, then we reached out after that meeting in New York and got the National Council of Churches, the AFL—not the AFL-CIO because George Meany never supported the march. Organized labor, per se, did not support the march. The AFL-CIO and Mr. Meany did not support the March on Washington. Was against the march, as a matter of fact. But Walter Reuther, as representative and head of the UAW, supported the march. The National Catholic Interracial Council supported the march, and the American Jewish Committee came in. So this brought in the white liberals, moderate, and a white element of, of organized labor under the gospel seed of UAW and Walter Reuther.

HAMPTON: Who was behind the movement to change your speech?

LEWIS: Well, from, from the outset it was, it was strange the way that happened, and to this day I don't know all what went to make that possible. We had, and when I say "we" I would say the representative of the Student Nonviolent Coordinating Committee, had assisted me in preparing what I thought was a very simple, very elementary statement for the March on Washington. Julian Bond was then the communication director of SNCC, had to make copies of the speech available in advance. The Tuesday night before the march, we all were staying at a hotel in Washington, DC, and that night I was in my hotel room. I got a call from Bayard Rustin who suggested that there was some problem with my speech and there would be a meeting to discuss the speech and other arrangements for the March on Washington and I should come down for the meeting. And at this meeting, there was representatives from SCLC, the NAACP, all of the organization, the Catholic Church, everybody. And we really argued about, about the speech.

HAMPTON: Well, who wanted you to change the speech?

LEWIS: Well, one suggestion was from a representative of the archbishop of the Diocese of Washington. See, during the early discussion with representatives of SNCC, SCLC, all of the organizations, it was never our design to come to Washington to support any particular piece of civil right legislation. But before the march—by the time we got to Washington—some of the people, particularly the representative of the Urban League, the NAACP, and maybe organized labor, that segment of organized labor, wanted the march to support a piece of legislation, a proposed legislation of President Kennedy. And we took exception to that. In one part of the speech, I suggested that we could not support the Kennedy legislation [because]—it did not guarantee the right of Black people to vote. Kennedy had suggested that a person with a sixth-grade education should be considered literate, and any literate person should be able to register to vote. And SNCC and I think the southern wing of the movement took the position that the only qualification for being able to register to vote should be that of age and residence. And during the time leading up to the preparation of my speech, there was an article in the *New York Times* with a group of women in, in Rhodesia, and they had signs saying ONE MAN, ONE VOTE. And in my speech, I said something like, "One man, one vote is the African cry. It is ours too, it must be ours." Some of the people objected to that. And another part of the speech where we suggested that, well, that there was very little difference between the major political parties. That the party of Javits is the party of Goldwater. That the party of Kennedy is the party of Eastland. Then I raised the question: Where is our party?

HAMPTON: How do you feel about that now?

LEWIS: Well, I still—somebody asked me about that just a day or so ago out in, in Compton, California. What about our party? It's—well, I still feel about the same way. Where's the party of the people? When you lo—well, that's a whole other discussion. But I suggested that, as a movement, that we could not wait on the president, on members of the Congress. We had to take matters into our own hand and went on to say that, that the day might come when we would not confine our marching on Washington, where we might be forced to march through the South the way Sherman did, nonviolently. And some of the people suggested that was inflammatory, that would call people to riot, and you shouldn't use that type of language. And Mr. Randolph, really, came to my defense—not that night, he was not present on that Tuesday night—but even after we got, after we arrived at the Lincoln Memorial, people had problems with some of the changes. The use of the word "revolution." I used "revolution" in it, the word "revolution" in the speech, at least once. The word "masses." Mr. Randolph said, "You know, I don't have any problem with 'revolution.' I don't have any problem with the word. I use them. I use those words myself sometimes." I said in, in one part of the speech, "We are involved in a serious revolution." I remember that very well. "The revolution is at, is at hand. The masses are on the march," or something like that. I don't—people, they couldn't deal with that. And it was, you know, it's nothing, you look back on it. And, and in 1965, all of that, what we tried to suggest in that speech on the concern of voting rights came to pass. The people in Selma, the people in Mississippi made it real through the Voting Rights Act. And, you know, all of the things that SNCC predicted and projected during that period came to pass in the Voter Rights Act of 1965. And—but for that, you know, day, it was, tended to be looked upon as being radical and extreme.

HAMPTON: When did you become aware that, that the march had—was shaping up to be kind of a lobby effort, specifically, for Kennedy's civil rights legislation?

LEWIS: I would say maybe a week or so before the march. Maybe two weeks before the march, yeah. See we, we had a, a short time to plan it. It was like from the first week in July to August 28th. And when the Kennedy Administration became so cooperative, when the, the people within the government became so helpful in providing logistic—the only thing they wanted, they wanted people to come in to Washington and to get out before sundown. They wanted all of the Black folks out of Washington before sundown and that's what—exactly what happened. People came in and they got out. And the, the afternoon, after the march, we went, went over to meet with President Kennedy. He congratulated the people, said— you know, I heard that someplace a few days ago that, as a matter of fact, that he really wanted to come by and speak, yeah.

HAMPTON: Do you know why he didn't speak?

LEWIS: No, I guess that—I don't, I don't know why. But several members of the Congress came and they took their seat right on the, on the steps of the Lincoln Memorial. Several. Over, over a hundred members of the Senate and the House came.

HAMPTON: Do you remember what persuaded the NAACP and the Urban League to participate in the march?

LEWIS: I think, perhaps more than anything, I think more than anything the NAACP, its membership. The youth membership and people at the, the base, local people, people in the South wanted to chart buses, get on trains, and come. I think more than anything, started putting pressure on the national office. With the Urban League, I think, Whitney Young happened to be sensitive to the mood and they saw the march—I think people had, they had a problem with SNCC, true enough, but they had problem also, real problems, with SCLC and, particularly, Dr. King. If I could tell you some stories and some meetings that—unbelievable. Leading up to the march in, in 1963. Another meeting in New York, I guess this was called the, the Unity, Civil Rights Unity Council, where—I have never before in my life seen a group of people—Dr. King hadn't made it to the meeting, but it was Mr. Wilkin [sic] who, you know, who's a good man, decent human being, and, and Whitney. I think James Farmer was there and, I think, our Jim, Jim Forman was there and maybe Floyd McKissick. But it was almost—it was the worst kind of red baiting I ever heard, I ever witnessed of, of Dr. King. It was like a conversation going on between Whitney and, and Mr. Wilkin [*sic*] about Martin. Saying, in the sense, that he was naïve, politically, and that he kept all of these sort of left people around him, and they thought that was bad, bad for the movement. And he was not politically in tune or sophisticated in it. But they had some problems with him, and apparently, during that whole period, and when I look back on it, I didn't know it at the time, but seeing what I've seen today in the Freedom of Information file and my own file and other thing, I'm sure, I'm convinced beyond a shadow of a doubt, that there was a great deal of sharing of information between the FBI, people within the Justice Department, between certain committees in the Congress, and people within the hierarchy of some of the old established civil rights organization. And they got information and—on different people—and then whether they used it or said, well, we understand that maybe you should get rid of a certain person. What representatives of the NAACP and Urban League were saying to Dr. King that you had to cut some people, cut certain staff people, cut some of your friends, some of your associates, because you're being tainted.

"WHEN I WAS ARRESTED, I FELT FREE"

INTERVIEW BY BRIAN LAMB
C-SPAN
JULY 11, 2012

BRIAN LAMB: Congressman John Lewis, why did you name your book *Across that Bridge*?

REP. JOHN LEWIS: Well, during the past few years, I've been crossing bridges, rivers, many bridges, bridges of understanding, building bridges, trying to bring people together to create what I like to call the beloved community.

LAMB: Where does the Edmund Pettus Bridge come into that picture?

LEWIS: Well, the Edmund Pettus Bridge is symbolic of so many bridges, but in 1965, when I was much younger, and head of an organization called the Student Nonviolent Coordinating Committee, a group of young people, students, and others attempted to cross the Edmund Pettus Bridge in Selma, Alabama, to march fifty miles from Selma to Montgomery to dramatize to the nation and to the world that people wanted simply to register to vote. We were walking in twos. And when we arrive at the apex of the bridge down below, we saw a sea of blue, Alabama state troopers. And we continued to walk.

And we came within hearing distance of the state troopers. And a man identified himself and said, "I'm Major John Cloud of the Alabama state troopers. This is an unlawful march. And it will not be allowed to continue." And one of the young people walking beside me said, "Major, give us a moment to kneel and pray." And the major said, "Troopers advance." And they came toward us, beating us with nightsticks and bullwhips, trampling us with horses, and releasing the tear gas.

At the foot of that bridge, I was beaten. I thought I was going to die. I thought I saw death. So at the foot of that bridge, I gave a little blood to make it possible for all people to be able to participate in a democratic process. So the book, it just a symbolic bridge of many bridges that we still must cross, rivers that we still must cross, before we build a beloved community, a truly democratic, multiracial society in America.

LAMB: Did you ever look up who Edmund Pettus was?

LEWIS: I did look up and discover this man, Edmund Pettus, a general in Alabama. You know, the bridge, this particular bridge, was dedicated the same year that I was born, in 1940. So I have a kinship to this bridge. And every year, sometime more than once a year, but every year, I make it a point to go back to that bridge and cross that bridge. And for the past forty-seven years, I've gone back the weekend—the first weekend in March—since 1965.

LAMB: How did it fit in with everything that was going on back in the sixties?

LEWIS: In order to travel from Montgomery to Selma, you had to cross that bridge. You had to cross the Alabama River. Selma was in the heart of the Black Belt of Alabama. That's where hundreds and thousands of poor, Black people lived. They had been sharecroppers. They had been tenant farmers.

But this little town, Selma, was a place of commerce. And people would come on a Friday and Saturday to shop. But in Selma, people could not register to vote simply because of the color of their skin. Only 2.1 percent of Blacks were registered to vote. You had to pass a so-called literacy test. On one occasion, a man was asked to count how many bubbles on a bar of soap. On another occasion, a man was asked to count the number of jelly beans in a jar. People stood in what I call unmovable lines. The only time you could even attempt to go down to the county courthouse and go up a set of steps to a set of double doors and get a copy of the so-called literacy test and the application was on the first and third Mondays of each month. And on occasion, the registrar would put up a sign saying the Office of the Registrar is closed. And people went there day in and day out, standing in line. People were beaten. Some arrested and jailed while they stood there.

LAMB: Today, the mayor of Selma is the second African American to have that job?

LEWIS: The mayor of Selma is the second African American mayor in that city. The city council is a biracial city council. The police chief is an African American. Selma is a different place today. It is a better place today.

LAMB: What happened to you after you were beaten? Where'd you go?

LEWIS: On that Sunday afternoon, I was beaten. And forty-seven years later, I don't recall how I made it back to the little church that we had left from. But apparently, someone literally carried me back to the church. I felt like I was going to die. I do recall, I thought I saw death. I really thought I was going to die.

But I do remember being back at that church, the little Brown Chapel at AME Church in downtown Selma. The church was full to capacity. More than two thousand people on the outside, trying to get in to protest what had happened on the bridge. And someone asked me to say something. And I stood up and said, "I don't understand it. I don't understand it. How President Johnson can send troops to Vietnam and cannot send troops to Selma, Alabama, to protect people whose only desire is to register to vote."

And the next thing I knew, along with sixteen other people, had been transferred to the local hospital in Selma, the Good Samaritan Hospital that was operated by a group of nuns. And these wonderful sisters, they took care of us. And today, many of those sisters are retired, living in Rochester, New York. And I plan to go there to visit them within the next few days.

LAMB: Anybody severely wounded, that they didn't get out of the hospital for a long time?

LEWIS: There were people who stayed for a few days, a few weeks. I got out within two days.

LAMB: Any of the names that were around you, would they be familiar to us, the people you marched with?

LEWIS: Well, I marched with—later, not on that day but later during the week and the following weeks—with Martin Luther King Jr. Dr. King came to the hospital to visit us the next day. And he said to me, he said, "John, don't worry. We'll make it from Selma to Montgomery." He told me that he had made an appeal for religious leaders to come to Selma. And two days later, more than a thousand priests, rabbis, nuns, and ministers came. And they marched to the same point where we had been beaten two days earlier.

And one young minister went out with a group that following Tuesday evening, to try to get something to eat at a local restaurant. They were attacked by members of the Klan. He was so severely beaten, the next day he died at a local hospital in Selma—in Birmingham, Alabama, rather. He was from Boston, Reverend James Reeb.

LAMB: So when was it that people could leave Selma, walk across the bridge, and go all the way to Montgomery and not get hassled?

LEWIS: We went into federal court and got an order against Sheriff Jim Clark, who was the sheriff of Selma and Dallas County, and against Governor George Wallace. And a federal judge issued an order saying that we had a right to march. President Lyndon Johnson came and spoke to a joint session of the Congress eight days after Bloody Sunday and condemned the violence in Selma, introduced the Voting Rights Act. And before he concluded that speech, he said, "And we shall overcome." We call it the "We Shall Overcome" speech. It probably was one of the most meaningful speeches any American president had delivered in modern time on the whole question of civil rights.

LAMB: On that note of we shall overcome, you mentioned in your book about Rosa Parks. And you go back to her training. You say that she wasn't trained—I mean that when she sat in that bus and wouldn't get up—that she had an earlier training for that in Tennessee. Can you tell us about that place?

LEWIS: There is a little school, at that time, a little school that exists in Tennessee in a little place called Mount Eagle, Tennessee. It is between Nashville and Chattanooga, Tennessee, and was called Highlander Folk School.

It was started by a guy, a brave and courageous white gentleman by the name of Myles Horton. It was a wonderful place, and he was a wonderful, wonderful man. It was to train and organize union people, many white workers. And then, he started working in a whole area of race relation, bringing Black people and white people together. It was one of the few meeting places in the heart of the Deep South, where Blacks and whites could meet. They start training people there how to organize, how to become community organizers, how to protest. And that's where we start singing

"We Shall Overcome." That's where Rosa Parks heard it. Rosa
Parks said it was the Highlander Folk School where she had
her first meal with someone of a different race.

It was also, for me, the first place that I had a meal with
someone white. But we worked together. We studied together.
And we studied the philosophy and the discipline of nonviolence. We studied what Gandhi attempted to do in South
Africa, what he accomplished in India. We studied what Dr.
Martin Luther King Jr. was all about in Montgomery. We
studied Thoreau and civil disobedience.

So we were prepared when the sit-ins came and the Freedom Ride. And by the time of Selma, we were more than
prepared.

LAMB: So Rosa Parks was in 1955, the bus incident.

LEWIS: Rosa Parks took a seat on December 1st, 1955, in
downtown Montgomery. And that led to the Montgomery
bus boycott of 1955 and '56.

LAMB: You'd have been fifteen then?

LEWIS: I was fifteen years old. And I remember like it was
yesterday. I heard about it on the radio. I read about it in a
local newspaper, but we were too poor to have a newspaper
subscription, but my grandfather had one. And when he were
finished reading his newspaper each day, we would get his
newspaper. And we would read his newspaper.

And I followed the drama of the Montgomery bus boycott. Now, when I was growing up, and visit the little town

of Troy, Alabama, or visit Tuskegee or visit Montgomery, and see those signs that said WHITE MEN, COLORED MEN, WHITE WOMEN, COLORED WOMEN, WHITE WAITING, COLORED WAITING, and asked my mother and my father, my grandparents, my great-grandparents why, why, they would say, "That's the way it is. Don't get in the way. Don't get in trouble."

But it was individuals like Rosa Parks and Martin Luther King Jr. and others that inspired me to get in trouble. And today, I call it good trouble, necessary trouble.

LAMB: You say in your book that you were in forty different prisons or forty different times you were behind bars. Can you tell us about some of those?

LEWIS: The first time I got arrested was in Nashville, Tennessee. I was a student there.

LAMB: At Fisk?

LEWIS: I was a student at Fisk. I first attended a little school called American Baptist College for four years and then Fisk for two years. I spent six years in Nashville. Nashville, Tennessee, was the first city that I lived in. I grew up in rural, rural Alabama. And going off to school there, I wanted to find a way to get in the way. I wanted to find a way to do something. When I heard Dr. King speaking on the radio, I felt like he was speaking directly to me, saying, "John Robert Lewis, you too can do something. You can make a contribution."

So going to Nashville and to Highlander Folk School prepared me to find a way. And I got involved in the sit-ins.

LAMB: How did you know about Highlander Folk School?

LEWIS: Attending meetings in Nashville, attending school, a church. And people would say you can go to Nashville. And from Nashville, you can go and visit Highlander Folk School. They're training people. They're teaching people. And when I got a chance to go with a group of my schoolmates and classmates, I made the trip there. And it was there that I literally grew up. It taught me how to be prepared to sit in. It taught me how to help organize. It—I grew up, I literally grew up at the age of eighteen and nineteen.

LAMB: Was Marion Barry* at Fisk when you were there?

LEWIS: Marion Barry was a graduate student at Fisk University when I was in Nashville. He attended some of the first nonviolent workshop. And he later became the chairperson of the Student Nonviolent Coordinating Committee, but he participated in the very first sit-in, the test sit-ins.

We had what we called test sit-ins in Nashville in the fall of 1959, students from Fisk University, Tennessee State University, Vanderbilt University, Peabody College, Meharry Medical College, and American Baptist. And we had just test the facilities, just establish the fact that we would be served or denied service. It was an interracial group of Black and white college students.

---

* Marion Barry was a member of the Nashville Student Movement and the first chairman of SNCC. He served as mayor of DC from 1979 to 1991 and again from 1995 to 1999.

LAMB: Why did you major in philosophy? And do you have a favorite philosopher?

LEWIS: I majored in philosophy. I was interested in becoming a minister. I studied philosophy and religion long before I went off to school. I had the desire, this burning desire. Some people call it a calling, that you're called to preach. You're moved by the Spirit, but I felt I needed to be trained.

When I was a little boy, I used to, from time to time, play church as a very, very, very young child. And it was my responsibility on the farm to care for the chickens, to raise the chickens. So we would gather all of our chickens together in the chicken yard. And my brothers and sisters and my cousins would help make up the audience, make up the congregation.

And I would start speaking or preaching. And when I look back, some of these chickens would bow their heads. Some of these chickens would shake their heads. They never quite said amen, but I'm convinced that some of those chickens that I preached to during the forties and the fifties tended to listen to me much better than some of my colleagues listen to me today. And some of those chickens was just a little more productive. At least, they produced eggs.

But those chickens taught me patience. And by the time I got to Nashville to school and the movement, I was prepared. I was ready to sit there, to sit in, to wait and wait all day into late evening to be served. And we were denied service. And we were arrested. And we went to jail.

The first time I got arrested was on February the 27, 1960. And when I was arrested, I felt free.

LAMB: Where did you go?

LEWIS: I was taken, placed in a wagon, and from that police wagon or van, taken to the city jail with eighty-eight other students.

LAMB: What's the longest time you ever spent in a prison?

LEWIS: The longest time I ever spent in a prison was in Mississippi.

LAMB: Parchman?

LEWIS: It was in Parchman. In Parchman, it was no one—no one in their right mind wanted to go to Parchman.

LAMB: Tell us about Parchman.

LEWIS: Parchman, you know, people are right about Parchman in novels, plays, poems. Parchman was known as sort of no-man's land. People go there and some people didn't return. I remember so well after staying many days in jail in Jackson, Mississippi, the city jail, the county jail, and then been taken down to Parchman.

LAMB: Were there others that we would know that were with you at the time?

LEWIS: One of the young people that went to jail with me in Parchman was Bob Filner. He was a congressperson from California. He was only nineteen years old. I was twenty-one at the time. But there was individuals like the Reverend James Lawson, became one of our wonderful teachers of the philosophy and discipline of nonviolence. Bernard LaFayette, James Bevel, Diane Nash, these were all young people in the movement. There were men and women that got arrested and went to jail. William Sloane Coffin got arrested and went to jail. There was lawyers, ministers, rabbis, priests. People came from all over the country. They couldn't take seeing people being arrested and taken to jail simply because they wanted to be served at a lunch counter or ride together on a bus.

LAMB: You didn't tell us who your favorite philosopher was?

LEWIS: My favorite philosopher when I was studying was Hegel. Hegel talked about the thesis—antithesis. He talked about the struggle between good and evil, that in society, if you're going to bring about change, there must be a struggle. And there must be a division between the forces of darkness and the forces of light, the forces of good and the forces of evil. And somehow, out of that evil and good, something wholesome must emerge. And in the final analysis, you got to move toward reconciliation.

So in the book, I talk about in the very last chapter, I talk about reconciliation. On the Freedom Rides in May of 1961, my seatmate was a young white gentleman. The two of us arrived at a little bus station in Rock Hill, South Carolina.

We were beaten, left bloody, left in a pool of blood. And one of the young men that beat me on May 9, 1961, came to my office in Washington in February '09.

LAMB: Elwin Wilson?

LEWIS: Yes, Elwin Wilson. Mr. Wilson came to my office with his son, who had been encouraging his father to seek out the people that he had abused and attacked during the sixties. He came and said, "Mr. Lewis, I'm one of the people that attacked you, that beat you. I want to apologize. Will you accept my apology? Will you forgive me?" He started crying. His son started crying. I started crying. He hugged me. I gave him a hug. He called me brother. I called him brother. And since then, I've seen the gentleman four more times. That was moving to a reconciliation.

And even today, when I go back to places in Alabama, other part of the South, young people and people not so young, some older people, white people of the South come up and say, "Mr. Lewis, Congressman Lewis, I want to apologize to you on behalf of all of the white people of Alabama of the South for what we did."

LAMB: Mr. Wilson and you were in confrontation physically where? He assaulted you where?

LEWIS: Mr. Wilson beat me, knocked me down, left me bloody at the Greyhound bus station in Rock Hill, South Carolina, which is about thirty-five miles from Charlotte, North Carolina.

LAMB: What was the occasion?

LEWIS: We were traveling through the South as part of the Freedom Riders, traveling on a Greyhound bus and some on a Trailway bus. Back in 1961, after you left Washington, DC, Black people and white people couldn't be seated together on a bus, couldn't use the same waiting room, couldn't be seated together at a lunch counter, or in a restaurant, couldn't use the same restroom facilities. We were testing a decision of the United States Supreme Court, trying to make it real. And people, not just in South Carolina, but in Alabama, people beat us at the Greyhound bus station in Montgomery, left us bloody and tried to bring down a church with hundreds of people in it that came to salute the Freedom Riders. And we rode on to Mississippi. And in Jackson, we were arrested, hundreds of us. We filled the city jail, the county jail. And later, we were transported to the state penitentiary at Parchman.

LAMB: How long were you in Parchman?

LEWIS: I was in Parchman for about forty days.

LAMB: What impact did it have on you?

LEWIS: Parchman gave me time to reflect, gave me time to contemplate, gave me the sense that I'm like a tree planted by the rivers of waters and I shall not be moved. It gave me a greater sense of determination and stick-to-it-ness that when I got out, I was going to continue to do what I could to end segregation and racial discrimination in the American South.

LAMB: You've been in Congress how many years?

LEWIS: I've been in Congress, at the end of this year would be twenty-six years.

LAMB: How did your autobiography do? We were last together and talking about that a number of years ago. It's still selling?

LEWIS: The autobiography, memoir, *Walking with the Wind*, it is still selling. It is doing very, very well. As a matter of fact, in many high schools and some colleges and universities around the country, it's required reading.

LAMB: Why did Mr. Wilson come back to reconcile with you? What triggered it?

LEWIS: More than anything else, I believe the election of President Barack Obama moved him, but it's also the influence of his son. His son wanted his father to be on the right side. And the father really wanted to be on the right side. This man is a wonderful, wonderful human being. He took a lot of heat for having the courage to do what he did, because the local press back in Rock Hill. And then, he was on national television. And so, people saw that, he got telephone calls.

But he's a brave and courageous man. He said it was the right thing to do. And he's very, very sincere. And he made me feel freer, and just meeting him, he was the very first person to come to me and apologize, really.

LAMB: I want to show you a different person in the movement. This goes back to 1966. And it's part of a speech that he gave. And I want to ask you the contrast, because you were both head of the Student Nonviolent Coordinating Committee. Let's watch this.

[*begin videotape*]

KWAME TURE (STOKELY CARMICHAEL):* If Black people control Lawrence County, they've got the tax assessor, or the tax collector, and the guns, the sheriff, they're going to raise the property tax. Since they don't own property in Lawrence County, white people either go sell or pay the taxes, and we can all go on welfare for a decent salary.

And it becomes crystal to me that if you have Black people who were responsive to the Manhattan, where they control it, since they're 60 percent, they can then begin to change the economy of that country. And the pressure that Black people will fight for will, in fact, motivate and move the rest of this country, because this country moves precisely because of the civil rights movement. That's why this country must stop it. Johnson must stop the civil rights movement because it is the biggest threat to his Great Society.

---

* Kwame Ture (born Stokely Carmichael) was a prominent organizer in the civil rights movement and the global Pan-African movement. He was a key leader in the Black Power movement, working to establish independent all-Black political organizations. The FBI flagged Ture as a potential "black messiah" and targeted him through COINTELPRO.

[end videotape]

LAMB: A man that looked at life a little bit differently than you did. Did you get along with him?

LEWIS: I got along with Stokely. He came south during the fall, late summer of 1961 during the Freedom Rides, and later came back during the Mississippi summer project in 1964. But I don't think Stokely ever understood the philosophy and the discipline of nonviolence. He never made that commitment.

He grew up in New York City, attended Howard University. And I think those of us who grew up in the heart of the Deep South, who came under the influence of Martin Luther King Jr. and individuals like Jim Lawson, who had a sort of a baptism in the philosophy and the discipline of nonviolence, we took the long, hard look. We believed that our struggle was not a struggle that lasts for a day or a few weeks or a few months or a semester. It was a struggle of a lifetime. And I said then, and I say it even today, that you have to pace yourself for the long, hard look, the long, hard struggle.

And you have to come to that point and accept nonviolence as a way of life, as a way of living. Our struggle was not a struggle between Blacks and whites, not a struggle between people, but a struggle between what is right and what is wrong, what is good, what is evil, between the forces of justice and the forces of injustice.

In the movement, during the time when I was chair of the Student Nonviolent Coordinating Committee, and in the movement itself in general, we call ourselves a circle of trust, a band of brothers and sisters. When someone got arrested with you, went to jail with you, someone beaten with you, almost died with you, you forget about race and color.

LAMB: How did the Student Nonviolent Coordinating Committee start? And who funded it in the early days? And where did it start?

LEWIS: The Student Nonviolent Coordinating Committee grew out of the sit-in movement. There was a young woman by the name of Ella Baker. She was not that young at the time, but she was young at heart.

LAMB: Now deceased?

LEWIS: Now deceased. She was working for Dr. Martin Luther King Jr. as his executive assistant in Atlanta at the Southern Christian Leadership Conference. And when the sit-in started spreading all across the South, like wildfire, Dr. King requested of her to call these young people together from the different college campus and have a conference. And she made the decision to hold this conference Easter weekend, April 1960, at Shaw University in Raleigh, North Carolina. And the reason she went to Shaw University, she knew the school because she was a graduate of Shaw University. She had worked for the NAACP. She had worked for the YWCA, for the NAACP. She was just one of these smart, gifted women that knew everybody. And she pulled this conference off. And all of these young people, but many, not just Black young people, but many young white people.

LAMB: Was she white or Black?

LEWIS: She was Black, but she had many, many allies in the white community, friends in the civic and social and religious organizations. And it was in that meeting that Dr. King thought that the students would become the youth arm or the student arm of his organization. But she insisted that we make up our own mind and create our own organization. So the organization were called the temporary Student Nonviolent Coordinating Committee. And Marion Barry, who had been a graduate student at Fisk University in Nashville, became the temporary chair of the temporary Student Nonviolent Coordinating Committee April of 1960. And later, there was a fall meeting in Atlanta on Morehouse College campus, where the Student Nonviolent Coordinating Committee became a permanent organization with Marion Barry as the chair of the organization.

James Clyburn, who is now in the Congress, was one of the students from South Carolina who attended the meeting with us in Atlanta in October 1960.

LAMB: And his daughter's now a member of the Federal Communications Committee?

LEWIS: His daughter is a member of the Federal Communications Commission.

LAMB: Do you—I want to show you some more video of Stokely Carmichael because I want to ask you what, years later, I think I did the last interview with him. And he died back in 1998, '99. His name then was Kwame Ture. And in this interview, you'll see I ask him about his career and all that. Let's watch a little bit of what he had to say. And tell us why he went one way and you went another?

[begin videotape]

CARMICHAEL: Both worked. You know, for me the difference here must clear between King and I, we started to talk about it before practicing the Black Power. But as we said, King took it as a principle, as a principle being an honest man, which he was, King had to use it all times under all conditions. For us, nonviolence was tactic, if you go back and look at some of your documentation, you will see me [being] nonviolent. I had been beaten. I had been sent to hospitals on nonviolent demonstrations. And I've never broken a non-violent demonstration. Only once in my life, and that was on the Mississippi March when the policeman pushed Dr. King have I ever broken the nonviolent discipline.

So I accept it, you know, but if it's no longer working now, I'm not going to, like Dr. King, to become hostage to what I consider to be a tactic as a principle. I'm going to pick up guns.

[end videotape]

LEWIS: I'm convinced that Stokely never, never, ever allowed himself to adhere to nonviolence as a way of life, as a way of living. He saw it only as a technique, only as a tactic as he said, only as a means to an end.

But those of us who accepted the philosophy of nonviolence as a way of life, as a way of living, we were saying in effect that means and ends are inseparable, that if you accept this idea that you're going to create the beloved community, if the beloved community is the end, if that is the goal, the methods, the means must be one of love, one of peace. And if you accept this idea that in the bosom of every creature, every human being, that there is this spark of what I call the divine, you don't have a right to abuse it. You respect the dignity and the worth of every person. And you— As Dr. King would say, hate, bitterness, is too heavy a burden to bare.

LAMB: Back in those early sixties, you talked a little bit about the Freedom Rides and about you being chairman of SNCC, the Student Nonviolent Coordinating Committee, for three years?

LEWIS: Yes, I served three long years as chair of the Student Nonviolent Coordinating Committee, longer than any other person.

LAMB: How big was the organization?

LEWIS: The organization had hundreds, hundreds of what we call members, and at one time they were staffers. But people were paid pennies. They were not people with big salaries.

Most of the individuals got like maybe ten dollars a week. And you got money for gasoline if you had a car and you had to drive some place, or if you had to fly some place.

But it was students from around the country and other organizations and individuals and groups that supported SNCC. It was a very poor organization.

LAMB: During your time, what's the biggest accomplishment you had?

LEWIS: During the time that I served as chair, it was during the March on Washington.

LAMB: How much did you have to do? I know you were standing on the steps there, and you were how old on that day?

LEWIS: I was twenty-three in 1963 when I became chair of the Student Nonviolent Coordinating Committee. And one of the first obligations that I had was to attend a meeting, along with Dr. Martin Luther King Jr. and several others with President Kennedy in June of 1963. And it was at that meeting that we told President Kennedy that we were going to march on Washington. I would never forget it. President Kennedy didn't like the idea of hundreds and thousands of people coming to Washington. He said, "If you bring all these people to Washington, won't there be violence and chaos and disorder? We'll never get a civil rights bill through the Congress."

And it was A. Philip Randolph, who we considered the dean of Black leadership, he was a labor leader, civil rights icon, really, he spoke up and said, "Mr. President, this will be an orderly, peaceful, nonviolent protest." And we went around the country organizing, mobilizing. And we invited four major white religious and labor leaders to join us in issuing the call for the March on Washington.

So there was ten of us that spoke and considered ourselves the leaders of the march. And I spoke number six. Dr. King spoke number ten. And out of the ten people that spoke that day, I know only one's still around.

But I remember so well after the march was over, after Dr. King had delivered that speech, President Kennedy invited us back down to the White House. He stood in the door of the Oval Office, greeting each one of us. He was like a beaming proud father. He was so glad that everything had gone so well. And he said, "You did a good job, you did a good job." And when he got to Dr. King, he said, "And you had a dream." It was my last time seeing President Kennedy.

LAMB: What's your reaction? This is not a positive, but what's your reaction to, over the years, the King family charging money for ability for somebody to look at the "I Have a Dream" speech?

LEWIS: I don't quite understand, I don't quite understand. I cannot make sense of that. No, the speech belongs to the ages. And I guess any of us could charge for someone reading or using the speech, but I don't know anyone doing anything like that. Would we charge someone for the Gettysburg Address, or some inaugural address by presidents? It's—or the State of the Union Address? That speech belongs to history.

LAMB: Do you have any idea why?

LEWIS: I have never been able to understand that. I really don't. I think it's heresy. I don't think Dr. King would be very pleased to know that his heirs charged for using his likeness or using his speech from an address.

LAMB: There's another person that I believe was chairman of the Student Nonviolent Coordinating [Committee], a guy named, named H. Rap Brown.*

LEWIS: H. Rap Brown, I never got really to know H. Rap Brown. He came long after I was no longer there. I made a decision when I was no longer the chair of the Student Nonviolent Coordinating Committee to leave because they laid down their commitment to the philosophy and to the discipline of nonviolence. And I didn't want to be associated with an organization or with a group that could not adhere and preach the philosophy.

LAMB: As you know, he's in prison for murder since 2000, but I want to show—his whole approach was even more agitating than Stokely Carmichael.

[begin videotape]

---

* Formerly known as H. Rap Brown, Jamil Abdullah Al-Amin was the fifth chairman of SNCC and former minister of justice for the Black Panther Party. He was targeted by the FBI's COINTELPRO and is currently serving a life sentence for murder after the shooting of two sheriff's deputies in Fulton County.

H. RAP BROWN: Lyndon Johnson, he can always raise an argument about law and order, because he never talks about justice, but Black people fall for that same argument. And they go around talking about law breakers. We did not make the laws in this country. We are neither morally, nor legally confined to those laws. Those laws that keep them up, keep us down. You've got to begin to understand that.

For four hundred years, he taught you white nationalism and you lapped it up. You taught it to your children. You had your children thinking that everything Black was bad. Black cows don't give good milk, Black hens don't lay eggs, Black for funerals, white for weddings. That's white nationalism. Santa Claus. A white honky who slides down a Black chimney and comes out white.

[end videotape]

LAMB: I have to say that last remark was interesting. "White honky who slides down a Black chimney comes out white."

LEWIS: There's a lot of rhetoric and there's a lot of playing on words and very emotional.

LAMB: Did it work?

LEWIS: That was not—that was not part of the SNCC that I knew.

LAMB: What happened?

LEWIS: Something went wrong. SNCC came to that point where, in my estimation, it was forced to die a natural death. We were conceived in this whole idea of the building of a truly interracial democracy. There were Black students and white students, working together, building together, suffering together. You cannot forget that in 1964, one year after I became chair, during the Mississippi summer project, that we recruited all these young people, Blacks and whites, primarily students, but lawyers, and doctors, and priests, and nuns came to work in Mississippi during the voter registration drive. That state had a Black vote in each population of more than 450,000, but only about 16,000 were registered to vote.

And these young people and people not so young came there to work in their freedom schools. And three young men that I knew, that I had met during the early part of the summer, Andy Goodman, Mickey Schwerner, white, James Cheney, African American, went out on a Sunday night, June 21, 1964. They were detained by the sheriff, later taken to jail. That same evening, they were taken from jail, beaten, shot, and killed. These three young men died there. Their bodies were discovered six weeks later. And you cannot forget that, that people suffered together, bled together, died together. And then, how can a movement make that radical jump by 1967 or 1968? And people like Stokely and Rap came to that point, where they were saying that all white people should leave SNCC, should leave and go and work in a white community. Our movement was an interracial movement. It was not to be a movement where we expel people, it was all-inclusive.

LAMB: By the way, in all of this, when did you meet your wife? Because I know you dedicated the book to her.

LEWIS: I met my wife at the end of 1967 at a dinner party, and we started dating.

LAMB: Where was the dinner party?

LEWIS: The dinner party was in Atlanta at a friend of her's home. And there was a discussion about the civil rights movement, about Dr. King and the movement. And she defended. She was a strong defender of the movement. And I guess that sort of warmed me toward her.

And she was wearing a beautiful dress. And it had the peace symbols. And I think that sort of grew me toward her. And I said to myself, this young lady believe in peace. And I don't know whether it was planned or whether it was a conspiracy on the part of the hosts of the party that she would defend the movement and that she would wear this dress with the peace symbol, but from that day on, we hit it off very well.

LAMB: She—You were twenty-seven. Were there people at that dinner party that were already against the movement?

LEWIS: Well, there was some people, not necessarily arguing against the movement, but there was some people questioning some of the tactics and techniques and where we were going. There were people, but she was a strong defendant.

She grew up in Los Angeles. She had never lived in the South. She had attended UCLA, USC. And she had spent two years in the Peace Corps. She studied to be a librarian. She came south to work at one of the university, at Atlanta University as a librarian. And she had a tremendous amount of interest in the civil rights movement.

LAMB: Do you have children?

LEWIS: We have one son. He's in Atlanta. He's taken a great deal of interest in music and also in politics, but he didn't want to run for any office.

LAMB: How much of Atlanta do you represent?

LEWIS: In the present district, I represent all of the city of Atlanta, the entire city. Well, most of the colleges, like Georgia Tech, Georgia State University, Morehouse, Spelman, Morris Brown, Clark, Atlanta University, but also represent Emory, CDC, major corporations are all in the district. It's a wonderful district, wonderful people.

LAMB: Let me read from your book in the introduction. "Remember how we thought the election of President Obama meant we had finally created a post-racial America, a place where the problems that have haunted us for a long—were finally silenced. Nobody says that anymore. We no longer dwell on that daydream. We were shaken to realism by the harshness of what we have witnessed in the last few years, the vilification of President Obama, the invisibility of the sick and poor murder at the Holocaust Museum and the shooting of Representative Gabrielle Giffords while she greeted constituents in a Safeway parking lot."

LEWIS: In spite of the election of President Barack Obama, we're not there yet. We made a lot of progress. His election, a major step down a very, very long road. But we have not yet created the beloved community.

People ask me all the time whether the election of President Barack Obama is the fulfillment of Dr. King's dream. I said, "No, it's just a down payment."

LAMB: How painful is it for you to look back in your support of Hillary Clinton over Barack Obama?

LEWIS: I don't feel any pain. I really don't feel any pain.

LAMB: What was the reason?

LEWIS: I knew President Clinton. I knew Hillary. I've known them long before I ever met President Barack Obama. And they had been friends of mine. They had been supporters of mine. President Clinton came to Atlanta, celebrated my birthday, my fiftieth. And President—Senator Obama came for my sixty-fifth. He was still in the Senate. But he's a good friend of mine. I'm still a good friend of President Clinton and Secretary of State Hillary Clinton and President Barack Obama. We're like a family.

And that's what the movement was all about. And we're one family. We're one people. We're one house. We may have our differences here or there, but we work through them.

LAMB: Let me read you another sentence. "The president of the United States was called a liar during a joint session of Congress at a State of the Union address. It was probably the lowest point of decorum I have witnessed in more than twenty years in the Congress."

LEWIS: It was unreal. It was unbelievable when I heard a member of Congress. It is just—you know, you have your differences. You have your feeling, but respect the office of the president if you cannot respect a man.

LAMB: Let me show you some videotape I found in our archives. Just a second.

[begin videotape]

REP. BARBARA LEE: President Clinton was impeached for lying about sexual involvement with an aide. Evidence has come into light that Bush and his administration have lied to the world. And to date, little is being done about it. I ask you, which infraction is more serious and warrants our time and money for investigation? Again, Lodi, California.

UNIDENTIFIED PARTICIPANT: The Chair would remind members that it is not an order to accuse the president of lying, or stating intentional falsehoods, even if by innuendo. Further, a member may not read into the record the remarks of others if they would be out of order as spoken by the member. Thank you.

REP. PETE STARK: But the—President Bush's statements about children's health shouldn't be taken any more seriously than his lies about the war in Iraq. The truth is that Bush just likes to blow things up.

UNIDENTIFIED PARTICIPANT: Members are reminded not to refer to the president in any personal way.

[end videotape]

LAMB: Both sides do it.

LEWIS: It is my hope that we all can come together and be a little more civil, be a little more human. That's what I'm trying to say in this book. Going back to Mr. Wilson, do we have the courage, do we have the power, do we have the ability, do we have the capacity sometime just to say, "I'm sorry, will you forgive me? Can we get along?"

Leaders must lead. You know, people around the nation, they see us on C-SPAN. And leaders must be a headlight and not a taillight.

LAMB: In the chapter "Peace," at the end, and we've got just a couple of minutes, I want to read a paragraph that you wrote and ask you how effective do you think it is to get people to read this? "I ask you to reach down inside yourself and find the truth your life is compelling you to see, that as you rode to true peace, and it is the beginning of the evolution of human kind, because every change in the world starts within. It begins with one individual, who envisions his or her microuniverse the way it can be and settles for nothing less. And as one individual moves toward the light, that light ignites more individual flames. And eventually, the revolutionary innerwork becomes a transformative outer work that builds into a bonfire of light, the kind of light that can change the world."

LEWIS: I believe that. I believe that one solitary individual, committed to the way of peace, the way of love, the way of nonviolence can change others, a community, a nation, a world. You have to—You know, we used to sing the little song during the movement, "This little light of mine/let it shine/I'm going to let it shine." We have to let our little light shine, not just in our little room, yes. Not just on Capitol Hill, yes, but in the larger world. And that's what we must do as a nation.

Somehow, we got to humanize our politics. Just be human. Humanize our institution. It's hard—it's difficult for elected officials to say, you know, I love you. Many of my colleagues in the Congress, I think people think it's strange sometime, I refer to them as brother. Hi, my brother. How are you doing, my brother? How are you doing, sister? Because I see us as a family. And we have to be examples to the larger nation, to the American community, and to the world.

LAMB: You wrote about Spencer Bachus in here, Republican from Alabama.

LEWIS: He's a wonderful human being.

LAMB: White?

LEWIS: He's white, represents part of Birmingham, Alabama. I've heard him tell stories, wonderful stories, about growing up, the role that his father played. We traveled together. Each year, when I take Black and white members, Republicans and Democrats, liberals, conservatives back to Alabama, he always hosts us. We travel together to India to remember the fifth anniversary of Dr. King's trip to India.

And he's my brother. He's my friend. He's more than a colleague.

LAMB: The name of the book, *Across That Bridge: Life Lessons and a Vision for Change.* Our guest has been United States Congressman John Lewis. Thank you very much.

LEWIS: Thank you very much. It's been an honor to be interviewed by you. Thank you.

THE LAST INTERVIEW: THE LONG VIEW: JOHN LEWIS, CONGRESSMAN AND CIVIL-RIGHTS LEGEND, WILL NEVER LOSE HOPE

INTERVIEW BY ZAK CHENEY-RICE
NEW YORK MAGAZINE
JUNE 8, 2020

John Lewis died on Friday from complications due to pancreatic cancer, an illness that divided the last few months of his life into "good days and days not so good," as he recently told me. He'd seen a lot in his eighty years—from a modest youth as the third of ten children in an Alabama sharecropping family, to a brutal and exhilarating early adulthood in the civil rights movement, to his storied tenure in Congress, where he represented Georgia's Fifth Congressional District from 1987 until his death. His later years were marked by novelty, much of it lamentable: the election of Donald Trump, who he believed was the worst president for civil rights in his lifetime, and his cancer diagnosis in December, less than a year before he had a chance to see Trump voted out of office. Neither the ups nor the downs much swayed his sense of optimism. Even its most recent test—the killing of George Floyd by Minneapolis police and the protests, rioting, and often violent police crackdown that followed—engendered in Lewis abundant cause for hope. Just over a month before his death, Lewis spoke to *New York* about why he'd stayed the course for so long, even as timeworn political strategies seemed inadequate to fixing urgent social problems, and he openly feared waking up one day to find that American democracy had disappeared. This instinct to be vigilant, but stubbornly hopeful, was, for many, among his most inspiring traits. He remains in death an example of what can be won if one is willing to make, in his words, "good trouble."

ZAK CHENEY-RICE: I'm curious, watching what's happened this past week or so, what has stood out to you?

REP. JOHN LEWIS: This determination of the young people, even not so young. Not just in America, but all around the world. I've come in contact with people who feel inspired. They're moved. They've just never been along in a protest—they've never been in a march before—they decided to march with their children and their grandchildren and great-grandchildren, and to walk with them. They're helping to educate and inspire another generation of activists. It's seeing an effect. There can be no turning back; there can be no giving up.

CHENEY-RICE: When you were protesting in the 1960s, was it an intentional strategy of yours to provoke white violence against yourself?

LEWIS: First of all, we believed in the philosophy and the discipline of nonviolence. We had attended nonviolence workshops. When we were beaten, arrested, and taken to jail, we never struck back. We said, if you're going to beat us, in effect, let it be in the daylight. So people can see what is happening. And we used our bodies as witness against segregation and racial discrimination. The philosophy of nonviolence became a way of life. A way of living.

When I was arrested the first time, in 1960, I felt free and I felt liberated. I felt like I had crossed over. And the local authority, the local officials, they couldn't fight us by putting us in jail. So we filled the city jails in Georgia, in Tennessee, and all around the South. And people around the country didn't like what they saw, seeing these young, well-dressed Black students being arrested and taken to jail.

What people did then, it appealed to the conscience of the American people. People couldn't take it. They couldn't understand it. Taking the beating and thrown in jail. People pouring hot water, hot coffee on us. We changed the attitude of hundreds of thousands of people.

CHENEY-RICE: It seems to me that the same kind of imagery is what's required today to spur action for a lot of people. Why do you think that is, more than fifty years later—that the most persuasive ways to create a sense of urgency for racial-justice causes is for lots of Americans to see images of Black people being beaten and harmed and killed?

LEWIS: Well, even today, I think people are moved all these many years later. They're moved and inspired to see people moving in an orderly, peaceful fashion. That people are willing to put their bodies on the lines for the cause.

CHENEY-RICE: One of the most striking things in the documentary is that you're very driven by your faith and a sense of optimism. When have you been most hopeless?

LEWIS: Studying and being trained in the philosophy and discipline of nonviolence, it helped to make me stronger, wiser, gave me a greater sense of determination, and if it hadn't been for my coming under the influence of Martin Luther King Jr., James Lawson, and wonderful, wonderful colleagues, students, the young people … I don't think I would have survived the beatings, the arrests. We became a family. We depended on each other. And if I had an opportunity to do it all over again, I would do it.

CHENEY-RICE: Have you had a moment where you felt that maybe this wasn't working?

LEWIS: No, I never ever came to that point. You get thrown in jail, maybe for a few days, and then you go to Mississippi, and you go to the state penitentiary, and you find some of your friends and your colleagues. And you get out, and you go on to the next effort. We used to say struggling is not a struggle that lasts for a few days, a few weeks, a few years. It is a struggle of a lifetime.

CHENEY-RICE: You mentioned when you were arrested, it was a liberating experience. From my experience with activists today, I don't get the sense that a lot of them feel the same way.

LEWIS: Well, no one in his or her right mind would like to be arrested and lose some freedoms or go to jail for a few days. But during the movement, we were taught it's part of the price that we would pay for trying to liberate our brothers and sisters, our mothers and fathers, our grandparents and great-grandparents.

CHENEY-RICE: Have you watched any of the videos that inspired the protests? For example, the video of Ahmaud Arbery being killed or the video of George Floyd being killed?

LEWIS: Yes, I have. Makes you cry. Makes you sick. You say to yourself, *How many more? How long? How long?* That's why I'm very hopeful. That's why I'm really optimistic about this upcoming election. [President Trump] cannot tell a lie over and over again when people have the photographs, the videos.

CHENEY-RICE: Do you think it's important for people to watch these videos? Or is it enough for them to just know what's contained in them?

LEWIS: I think it's important for some people. All of the people cannot take it. They become bitter, hostile. Some of them just give up; they drop out. I kept hearing people saying, "I can't take it any longer. I can't take it anymore."

CHENEY-RICE: Do you ever get angry about this stuff?

LEWIS: No, I don't get what I call angry. Every so often, I have a sense of righteous indignation, and I just feel like if I was the same John Lewis as John Lewis a few years ago, I would be out in the street.

CHENEY-RICE: What do you do to keep from becoming bitter?

LEWIS: I pray over and over again, have what I call an executive session with myself, just self-listen: *This is what you must do. This is what you must say. Do what you can, and play the role that you can play.*

CHENEY-RICE: So much of your life's work has been dedicated to advocating for the importance of voting and effecting legislation to end racial inequality. And yet racist violence at the hands of law enforcement is a constant, really, no matter which political party is in power. How much of these problems is it possible to solve through voting and legislation?

LEWIS: A great many of these problems we'll be able to solve through the power of the ballot. The vote is the most powerful nonviolent tool we have in a democratic society. And it's why people didn't want people of color to come register to vote, because you have power that you can use.

CHENEY-RICE: We have, in a lot of the cities where this unrest is happening today, progressive mayors, progressive city councils, and yet law-enforcement violence occurs regardless of who's in office. I just wonder: Where should concerned Americans be directing their energy when voting the right people, or who they think are the right people, into office doesn't seem to be solving the problem?

LEWIS: We must never ever give up, or give in, or throw in the towel. We must continue to press on! And be prepared to do what we can to help educate people, to motivate people, to inspire people to stay engaged, to stay involved, and to not lose their sense of hope. We must continue to say we're one people. We're one family. We all live in the same house. Not just an American house but the world house. As Dr. King said over and over again, "We must learn to live together as brothers and sisters. If not, we will perish as fools."

CHENEY-RICE: Do you have any advice or thoughts for communities that are looking for ways to reform how policing is done where they live?

LEWIS: It is my belief that we must work on a national level as well as a local level. That we need to humanize police forces, humanize the people, whoever is in charge of the police department at the local level but also at the national level.

CHENEY-RICE: Can you tell me what you mean by "humanize"? Do you mean we need to understand that they are humans too?

LEWIS: Well, I mean that we all are human beings, and we must be treated like human beings and respect the dignity and the way of each other. What happened in Atlanta with the officer beating up two young students was uncalled for. And I think the mayor and the police chief did the right thing, and they didn't wait—they did it right on the spot. Of course, officers of the law didn't have a right to abuse other people's right. You have to be human.

CHENEY-RICE: Do you think there are major philosophical differences between the way that your generation viewed the struggle for civil rights and the way today's younger generation views it?

LEWIS: Well, I wouldn't say there are major differences. I think my generation of young people was greatly influenced by the teachings of Martin Luther King Jr. and by individuals like James Lawson. And we dedicated ourselves to creating what we called the loving community. We wanted to do what we called "redeem the soul of America." We wanted to save America from herself.

CHENEY-RICE: The fact that you bring up restoring the soul of America is very interesting, because that's similar to one of the major slogans for Joe Biden's campaign for president. At the same time, he's been running a campaign promising to return things to normal or the sense of normal that existed before President Trump. Is this a message that Democrats should be running on right now? A return to normal?

LEWIS: I think Democrats should be preaching a message of hope, that we are going to inject something a little more meaningful into the very vein of our politics, into the very vein of our Democratic ideas, and make it possible for people to be a little more human, humanize our government, humanize our politics.

CHENEY-RICE: It's become clear, especially in recent years, that the task of legislating can be a very, very slow process.

And depending on how strong your opposition is, it can be almost impossible for long stretches of time. Did you ever feel that you made faster progress as an activist than you do as a legislator?

LEWIS: Oh yes. You have to find ways from time to time to dramatize, to make real the process that we're in the process of making. You have to find ways to inspire, educate, and change people. And you have to continue to center people.

CHENEY-RICE: Do you ever have regrets about making the jump from pure activism to becoming an elected official yourself?

LEWIS: No, I don't have any regrets. I feel sometimes that there's much more that we can do, but we've got to organize ourselves and continue to preach the politics of hope, and then follow our young people, who will help us get there. And we will get there. We will redeem the soul of America. We will create the loving community in spite of all of the things that we witness. The past few days, it made me very sad. There were times I wanted to cry, but the tears wouldn't come.

CHENEY-RICE: The signature legislative accomplishment that you're most associated with was before your time in Congress—the Voting Rights Act of 1965.

LEWIS: I'm very, very proud that I played a role in helping to get the Voting Rights Act of 1965 passed.

CHENEY-RICE: Having been so involved in the push for voting rights, what was it like for you personally to see the Voting Rights Act get the treatment that it got by the Supreme Court in 2013, with the elimination of the preclearance formula?

LEWIS: Well, it made me very sad. I gave a little blood on that bridge in Selma to get the Voting Rights Act passed. But things are going to change again. I'm convinced that we have the ability, we have the capacity, to hold on to the House and take the Senate.

CHENEY-RICE: Looking at the language of the Voting Rights Act, do you think there were any flaws in its original writing that prevented it from being more resilient against the attacks it has faced recently?

LEWIS: Well, I think the original drafters of the act, those members were trying to get a bill through Congress that would be supported by the majority. But we need to fix it. My idea back then was "one person, one vote." Make it simple. Make it easy.

CHENEY-RICE: Does that mean no Electoral College?

LEWIS: Well, if it was left up to me, there wouldn't be one.

CHENEY-RICE: Since the Voting Rights Act was passed, you've seen a lot of presidents come and go. Who do you think has been the worst president for civil rights since the 1960s?

LEWIS: The worst president for civil rights since the 1960s? Without a doubt, it is this president.

CHENEY-RICE: President Trump?

LEWIS: Yes. Without a doubt. I don't think there's any debate there.

CHENEY-RICE: He's only been in office for three years. It seems like he hasn't had nearly as much time as, say, Nixon or Reagan.

LEWIS: Well, he's been uncaring, insensitive to the problems and issues in front of him, especially when it comes to issues of civil rights.

CHENEY-RICE: Is there another president who comes close?

LEWIS: I couldn't name another one that comes close.

CHENEY-RICE: Wow.

LEWIS: I wouldn't put anyone close to him.

CHENEY-RICE: What are you most worried about if Trump wins in November?

LEWIS: Well, I must tell you, I don't worry about it because I truly believe that he cannot and will not win. People can only take it so long.

CHENEY-RICE: How worried are you about voter suppression in November?

LEWIS: I am concerned. I think there will be some attempt to oppress voters, but to steal elections, I don't think they'll get away with it.

CHENEY-RICE: What makes you so optimistic when Trump has already won once and when voter suppression has been used successfully, at least at the state level, for the past ten years?

LEWIS: Well, I'm convinced a great majority of people are watching what is happening, how it's happening. I think the word will go out that people are watching, and you cannot get away on this one.

CHENEY-RICE: The Republican Party seems to have become a party that is largely uninterested in governing in a bipartisan way. What does this tell you about the future of bipartisan legislating?

LEWIS: It may be almost impossible. But the way things look now, I think we're gonna pick up seats in the House, become a greater Democratic majority. And I believe we will take the Senate back. Then we should be a more effective body.

CHENEY-RICE: Do you think that reparations are on the table and politically possible once that happens?

LEWIS: I think it is a piece of legislation that will be considered, and there will be support for it. It could take time to educate enough people and get enough members that will be committed, and in Senate quarters, there'll be strong opposition. But it's something that we need to put on the House floor, and the Senate's floor, and debate. In light of what has happened in the past—I tell ya, people should be prepared and ready to engage in a debate.

CHENEY-RICE: What has been your most hopeful moment as a legislator? The time when you think things have come the closest to the vision that you were advancing when you were an activist?

LEWIS: Well, the chance to pass legislation to recognize the contribution of Dr. Martin Luther King Jr.—I think that was a major accomplishment, making Dr. King's birthday a national holiday. For all of the schoolchildren all over America, to many people around the world, they would know that this young African American made a major contribution to have set the American house in order.

CHENEY-RICE: The price of his incorporation into mainstream reverence has been a lot of misuse of his legacy. I wonder what you think about the fact that anytime there is a peaceful, nonviolent racial-justice protest, there are a lot of people who use Martin Luther King as a cudgel against protesters, saying, "Dr. King wouldn't have wanted you to do this because it is drawing attention to issues that divide people instead of bring them together."

LEWIS: That Martin Luther King Jr. believed in action. He believed in people being engaged. He believed in people carrying the ability to say "yes" when they may have the desire to say "no." He preached the philosophy of nonviolence, but he also was a man of action.

CHENEY-RICE: I'm sure you've seen that President Trump has become increasingly authoritarian in regard to the protests, with his threats of deploying the military. What do you think Congress's role is in keeping protesters safe from him, and what solutions are you and your colleagues considering?

LEWIS: Well, I know there are ongoing discussions right now about what role we should play and what we should set in motion to protect the human rights and legal rights of all of our citizens.

CHENEY-RICE: Can you give any details on what those involve?

LEWIS: No. It's still in its early stages. People are still discussing it.

CHENEY-RICE: I know that a lot of the younger members of Congress really look up to you and have reached out to you for advice. Can you tell me what those conversations look like? Who has impressed you the most from this younger generation, people like Alexandria Ocasio-Cortez, Ilhan Omar, Ayanna Pressley?

LEWIS: Well, I shouldn't get into the business of naming names. Many of these people that are young, and some not so young, we've become friends. We talk over the telephone, on the floor of the House, different times and places. They're so smart. They're so gifted. Their minds are their own; they know where they're going. Sometimes I feel like saying, "Pace yourself. It's all going to work out. Don't burn out." They're in a hurry, and we all should be in a hurry. We don't have time to waste.

In my younger days, I said, "You tell us to wait and tell us to be patient. It cannot wait. We cannot be patient. We want our freedom, and we want it now." And so, when I hear the young people, it's not new for me. It's very inspiring and uplifting. I think we need people to come along every so often who have the energy and the fire to push and pull.

CHENEY-RICE: Have any of them come to you to talk about their frustrations with maybe not being able to move the party in the direction that they wanted to move in?

LEWIS: Well, young members come and talk and I listen. From time to time, on some issues, I may say, "Go with your gut. Go with your conscience. Don't burn yourself out. We have to live with the decisions we made."

CHENEY-RICE: What do you say to people who have decided that the two-party system of voting doesn't accomplish the goal of ending racial inequality?

LEWIS: My recommendation is don't give up on the party, hang in there, and let's have changes from the inside. Become a leader in the party and organize other people to become leaders, to make the party more progressive, more liberal.

CHENEY-RICE: You mentioned in the film, I think, that sometimes you fear that you'll go to sleep and wake up and our democracy will be gone.

LEWIS: Oh yeah. Oh yeah.

CHENEY-RICE: How do you think you'll know when it's gone? It seems like there are so many signs day by day that it's going or it's close to gone. And for a lot of people, in many ways, it is gone.

LEWIS: Well, we must not allow that to happen, but you have someone in the White House like we have today, taking the position that he's taken, and taking us back to another time, to another place. We've come too far, we've made too much progress, to slow down or to go back. So we must go forward.

CHENEY-RICE: I know that you're going through some difficult times in regard to your health. I'd be interested to know how you're feeling.

LEWIS: Well, my health is improving. I'm feeling good. I'm doing better. And I'm going to continue to listen to the doctor and try to eat right and get enough rest and sleep. But I have good days and days not so good. But I feel good today.

CHENEY-RICE: I'm very glad to hear that. I wonder what you think you can realistically hope to see change in your lifetime around issues of racism and racial inequality?

LEWIS: Well, I hope the day will come when we will see more people of color, more women, elected to higher and more responsible positions. And I think it will happen. To have women, to have Hispanic, Asian American, and especially African Americans, in places of high responsibility is going to help educate, sensitize, and make a better country and a stronger country.

CHENEY-RICE: Do you think activists today should approach these issues more with your attitude, or are some people needed who are less patient and who approach these issues much more confrontationally?

LEWIS: Well, I think we need the energy, the commitment and dedication, of all people, but especially young people. And people of a certain age, they're much more willing to push and pull and not give up or throw in the towel. But there's roles for people to play, and we should never ever give up on the different roles that we can play. Some individuals can play one role much better than others.

JOHN LEWIS (1940–2020) was a civil rights activist and US congressman. Inspired by the activism of Martin Luther King Jr., Lewis became involved in the civil rights movement by participating in lunch counter sit-ins as part of the Nashville Student Movement and went on to become one of the original Freedom Riders in 1961. A founding member of the Student Nonviolent Coordinating Committee, he became its chairman in 1963, was an organizer of the infamous Bloody Sunday march on the Edmund Pettus Bridge in Selma, Alabama, and was a speaker at the March on Washington. Elected to Congress in 1986, Lewis served seventeen terms, representing most of Atlanta, Georgia. He received the Presidential Medal of Freedom in 2011.

JELANI COBB is a staff writer for *The New Yorker* and the Ira A. Lipman Professor of Journalism at Columbia Journalism School. His most recent book is *The Substance of Hope: Barack Obama and the Paradox of Progress.*

PETER A. HALL was one of the first Black lawyers in Birmingham, Alabama, and became Birmingham's first Black judge in 1972. He served as the local counsel for the NAACP Legal Defense and Educational Fund and was a founding member of the Alabama Black Lawyers Association.

JACK GREENBERG (1924–2016) was an attorney and legal scholar who served as the Director-Counsel of the NAACP Legal Defense and Educational Fund from 1961–1984. He argued forty civil rights cases in front of the US Supreme Court, including *Brown v. Board of Education* and *Meredith v. Fair.* He was an Alphonse Fletcher Jr Professor of Law Emeritus at Columbia Law School and was awarded a Presidential Citizens Medal in 2001.

NORMAN AMAKER (1935–2000) was an attorney and legal scholar. He spent ten years working with the NAACP Legal Defense and Educational Fund after being hired by Thurgood Marshall. Beginning in 1971, he served as executive director of the Neighborhood Legal Services Program in Washington, DC, before joining the faculty at Loyola University in 1976. In the early 1990s, Amaker founded the Midwestern People of Color Legal Scholarship Conference to provide mentoring and feedback to the scholarly writings of law professors of color.

CHARLES H. JONES, JR., was an NAACP Legal Defense and Educational Fund lawyer.

MAURY D. SMITH served as an assistant state attorney general and a deputy district attorney for Montgomery County.

W. MCLEAN PITTS was a prominent attorney in Selma, Alabama.

HENRY HAMPTON (1940–1998) was a filmmaker who founded Blackside, Inc., in 1968, three years after he participated in the Selma march in 1965. Blackside became the largest Black-owned film company from the mid-1970s until the late 1990s. Hampton produced over eighty programs, including *Eyes on the Prize* and *The Great Depression*. He received seven Emmys, an Academy Award nomination, and multiple Peabody Awards.

BRIAN LAMB is a journalist and founding CEO and executive chairman of C-SPAN. Prior to C-SPAN, he was a White House telecommunications policy staffer and Washington bureau chief for *Cablevision*. He has received the Presidential Medal of Freedom and the National Humanities Medal.

ZAK CHENEY-RICE is a staff writer at *New York Magazine* where he covers race and inequality for Intelligencer, the publication's digital politics vertical. His analysis-based work focuses on how race affects elections, policy, and the criminal-legal system.

THE LAST INTERVIEW SERIES

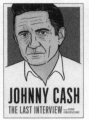

JOHNNY CASH:
THE LAST INTERVIEW

$16.99 / $21.99 CAN

978-1-61219-893-4
ebook: 978-1-61219-894-1

FRIDA KAHLO:
THE LAST INTERVIEW

$16.99 / $21.99 CAN

978-1-61219-875-0
ebook: 978-1-61219-876-7

FRED ROGERS:
THE LAST INTERVIEW

$16.99 / $21.99 CAN

978-1-61219-895-8
ebook: 978-1-61219-896-5

TONI MORRISON:
THE LAST INTERVIEW

$16.99 / $21.99 CAN

978-1-61219-873-6
ebook: 978-1-61219-874-3

SHIRLEY CHISHOLM:
THE LAST INTERVIEW

$16.99 / $21.99 CAN

978-1-61219-897-2
ebook: 978-1-61219-898-9

GRAHAM GREENE:
THE LAST INTERVIEW

$16.99 / $21.99 CAN

978-1-61219-814-9
ebook: 978-1-61219-815-6

RUTH BADER GINSBURG:
THE LAST INTERVIEW

$17.99 / $22.99 CAN

978-1-61219-919-1
ebook: 978-1-61219-920-7

URSULA K. LE GUIN:
THE LAST INTERVIEW

$16.99 / $21.99 CAN

978-1-61219-779-1
ebook: 978-1-61219-780-7

THE LAST INTERVIEW SERIES

**JULIA CHILD:
THE LAST INTERVIEW**

$16.99 / $22.99 CAN

978-1-61219-733-3
ebook: 978-1-61219-734-0

978-1-61219-733-3
ebook: 978-1-61219-734-0

**HANNAH ARENDT:
THE LAST INTERVIEW**

$15.95 / $15.95 CAN

978-1-61219-311-3
ebook: 978-1-61219-312-0

**KURT VONNEGUT:
THE LAST INTERVIEW**

$15.95 / $17.95 CAN

978-1-61219-090-7
ebook: 978-1-61219-091-4

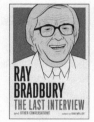

**RAY BRADBURY:
THE LAST INTERVIEW**

$15.95 / $15.95 CAN

978-1-61219-421-9
ebook: 978-1-61219-422-6

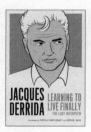

**JACQUES DERRIDA:
THE LAST INTERVIEW:
LEARNING TO LIVE
FINALLY**

$15.95 / $17.95 CAN

978-1-61219-094-5
ebook: 978-1-61219-032-7

**JAMES BALDWIN:
THE LAST INTERVIEW**

$15.95 / $15.95 CAN

978-1-61219-400-4
ebook: 978-1-61219-401-1

**ROBERTO BOLAÑO:
THE LAST INTERVIEW**

$15.95 / $17.95 CAN

978-1-61219-095-2
ebook: 978-1-61219-033-4

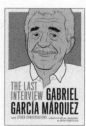

**GABRIEL GÁRCIA
MÁRQUEZ: THE LAST
INTERVIEW**

$15.95 / $15.95 CAN

978-1-61219-480-6
ebook: 978-1-61219-481-3

THE LAST INTERVIEW SERIES

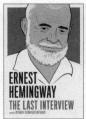

ERNEST HEMINGWAY:
THE LAST INTERVIEW

$15.95 / $20.95 CAN

978-1-61219-522-3
ebook: 978-1-61219-523-0

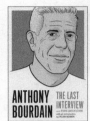

ANTHONY BOURDAIN:
THE LAST INTERVIEW

$16.99 / $22.99 CAN

978-1-61219-824-8
ebook: 978-1-61219-825-5

PHILIP K. DICK:
THE LAST INTERVIEW

$15.95 / $20.95 CAN

978-1-61219-526-1
ebook: 978-1-61219-527-8

MARTIN LUTHER KING, JR.:
THE LAST INTERVIEW

$15.99 / $21.99 CAN

978-1-61219-616-9
ebook: 978-1-61219-617-6

NORA EPHRON:
THE LAST INTERVIEW

$15.95 / $20.95 CAN

978-1-61219-524-7
ebook: 978-1-61219-525-4

CHRISTOPHER HITCHENS:
THE LAST INTERVIEW

$15.99 / $20.99 CAN

978-1-61219-672-5
ebook: 978-1-61219-673-2

JANE JACOBS:
THE LAST INTERVIEW

$15.95 / $20.95 CAN

978-1-61219-534-6
ebook: 978-1-61219-535-3

HUNTER S. THOMPSON:
THE LAST INTERVIEW

$15.99 / $20.99 CAN

978-1-61219-693-0
ebook: 978-1-61219-694-7

THE LAST INTERVIEW SERIES

BILLIE HOLIDAY:
THE LAST INTERVIEW

$16.99 / $21.99 CAN

978-1-61219-741-8
ebook: 978-1-61219-742-5

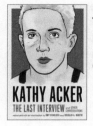

KATHY ACKER:
THE LAST INTERVIEW

$15.95 / $20.99 CAN

978-1-61219-731-9
ebook: 978-1-61219-732-6

JORGE LUIS BORGES:
THE LAST INTERVIEW

$15.95 / $17.95 CAN

978-1-61219-204-8
ebook: 978-1-61219-205-5

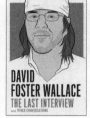

DAVID FOSTER WALLACE:
THE LAST INTERVIEW

$16.99 / $21.99 CAN

978-1-61219-741-8
ebook: 978-1-61219-742-5

DAVID BOWIE:
THE LAST INTERVIEW

$16.99 / $22.99 CAN

978-1-61219-575-9
ebook: 978-1-61219-576-6

MARILYN MONROE:
THE LAST INTERVIEW

$16.99 / $21.99 CAN

978-1-61219-877-4
ebook: 978-1-61219-878-1

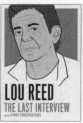

LOU REED:
THE LAST INTERVIEW

$15.95 / $15.95 CAN

978-1-61219-478-3
ebook: 978-1-61219-479-0

PRINCE:
THE LAST INTERVIEW

$16.99 / $22.99 CAN

978-1-61219-745-6
ebook: 978-1-61219-746-3